Becoming Fraud Wise

A Practical Guide to Digital Safety:
Spotting and Stopping Scams & Schemes

By

Emily Hicks, CFE

Published by

 FRAUD SAFE
COLLECTIVE

Becoming Fraud Wise
A Practical Guide to Digital Safety: Spotting and Stopping Scams & Schemes
Copyright © 2025 by Emily Hicks. All rights reserved.

Published 2025 by Fraud Safe Collective
Atlanta, GA
www.fraudsafecollective.com

ISBN: 979-8-9932953-2-9
Library of Congress Control Number: 2025920949

Text, original composition, and cover design by Emily Hicks.
Some original photos by author. Some images/graphics used under license from and in compliance with Pexels.com; some images/graphics used under license from and in compliance with Vecteezy.com. Both allow modification and commercial use without attribution.
Logo design by Barbara Hicks, B-Graphic.

First Edition
Designated as the 2026 Edition

For Roger and Donna, my loving parents,
who gave me the gifts of goals and dreams and the ability to realize them.

when
you
know *better,*
you
do *better*

CONTENTS

PREFACE

In a world where attention spans are short – and email, calls & texts come quick – staying alert to scams and schemes is essential. Fraud evolves as fast as technology yet planning and protection strategies aren't always top of mind. Throughout my law enforcement career, I've made it a priority to share what I've learned with family and friends—and I'm honored to now share that knowledge with you.

The truth is simple: scammers only need to be right once; we have to avoid their traps every single time. Statistically, that's not likely without preparation. These days, if you fail to plan you plan to fail.

This guide provides practical tools to build strong security habits and empower you to be the smartest one in the room with easily applied strategies. It will instill a default of situational awareness – which will be your mindset and serve you well.

Confidence comes from preparation. With the right mindset and everyday habits, every family member – from kids to seniors – can feel capable and secure.

If investing in yourself is always the power move, you've made a wise commitment in protecting yourself and the people in your world. When we know better, we do better – knowledge truly is power!

Emily

INTRODUCTION

Fraud and scams have become increasingly sophisticated in our digital age. Every year, millions of people fall victim to various schemes designed to steal money, personal information, or both. Building upon our knowledge is akin to building our very own personal firewall.

This guide is designed to help you recognize the warning signs and protect yourself and your families from the most common fraud tactics. Combatting the ever-changing barrage of scams takes a village; share your insights not only with your nuclear family, but with your friend family, your church family, your work family, your neighbor family – so every family can be fraud wise.

MY *story*

I'm Emily, a Certified Fraud Examiner and former federal investigator, and my goal is to share what I've learned about scams, fraud schemes, and digital safety to help you protect the people in your world – especially teens, tweens and seniors. It was borne from a career in law enforcement, where I got my start at the age of 19.

I became a seasoned member of a local police department and the Massachusetts State Police while I worked my way through Northeastern University to a Bachelor of Science degree in Criminal Justice. Those roles led to many rewarding years in federal service. I served in public health emergency response coordination leading CDC responses to a Marburg outbreak, the Indonesian tsunami and Hurricane Katrina, among others. I spent 20+ years in the inspector general community investigating fraud, waste, abuse, mismanagement and ethics. I investigated 9/11 fraud with FEMA-OIG and DHS-OIG, and the manslaughter side of the Deepwater Horizon oil rig disaster with DOI-OIG, among countless other cases. I've received numerous awards for my work, and am a credentialed member of the Association of Certified Fraud Examiners.

My work has contributed to >670 federal investigations and:

- 113 criminal convictions
- 258 years imprisonment
- 344 years' probation
- $4.6 billion in fines
- $20.1 billion in civil penalties & settlements
- $30.5 million in government restitution
- 134 personnel actions
- 74 government contractor suspensions & debarments
- Active engagement in dozens of disaster declarations & federal emergency response activations
- Thousands of local & state 911 calls answered, triaged, & responses managed

I believe in leveraging the power of people, data and tools in service of others.

MY

To empower individuals and families to recognize, prevent, and respond to scams by providing practical tools, clear education, and a supportive community that fosters digital safety and confidence.

mission

MY

I value trust, transparency, empowerment, and integrity. I believe that knowledge shared is protection gained, and I am committed to creating a safe space where families can learn, stay informed, and safeguard one another in an ever-changing digital world.

value

FRAUD-SAFE VALUES

TRUST

Trust means creating confidence that information, guidance, and actions are reliable and honest. It is built through consistency, transparency, and always putting the well-being of others first.

TRANSPARENCY

Transparency is being open and clear about intentions, decisions, and information so there is no confusion or hidden agenda. It builds accountability and strengthens relationships by ensuring people know they can rely on honest communication.

EMPOWERMENT

Empowerment is giving people the knowledge, tools, and confidence they need to make informed decisions and protect themselves. It encourages independence and resilience by showing that everyone has the ability to take control of their safety and well-being.

INTEGRITY

Integrity is the commitment to act with honesty, fairness, and consistency, even when no one is watching. It builds lasting credibility by ensuring that words, actions, and values always align.

CHAPTER

01

THE PREPARED MINDSET

In today's hyper-connected world, scams and fraud are no longer rare occurrences—they're persistent threats that evolve as quickly as technology does. Developing a prepared mindset means cultivating awareness, skepticism, and a proactive approach to digital interactions. It's about recognizing red flags before they escalate: unsolicited messages, urgent requests, unfamiliar links, and too-good-to-be-true offers. A prepared mindset isn't paranoid—it's informed. It empowers individuals to pause, verify, and protect themselves and their personal information with confidence. Prevention starts with education and vigilance. By staying updated on common scam tactics and understanding how fraudsters manipulate trust, people can build digital resilience. Whether it's learning to spot phishing attempts, securing accounts with multi-factor authentication, or simply knowing when to say "no," a prepared mindset transforms passive users into active defenders. In a landscape where deception is designed to feel familiar, preparation is the strongest safeguard.

Who's behind all these scams?

Scammers can be located in the US or anywhere in the world. Computer connectivity allows them to attempt scams quickly – generate emails, call or text your phone, sound like someone you know, even ship a box to your door.

Many of these communications are computer generated and only engage if you answer the phone or respond to their text – that's how quick it is. They're designed to look like legitimate business but with a goal of starting a conversation or installing malware.

Who exactly are they?

- Organized crime groups
- Small-scale domestic scammers
- Corrupt "click farms" & fraud factories
- Cybercriminal hackers
- Insiders & trusted people (caregivers, family members, employees)
- State-sponsored or political actors, including other governments

It's not about "exactly which country" or "which gang" — it's that scammers are highly organized, motivated, and relentless. They work like businesses, with strategies, teams, and quotas.

Q. Why is it so hard to catch them or get defrauded money back?

A. Scammers operate internationally using untraceable tools and programs; due process creates legal barriers to catching people using fast and disposable tactics, and law enforcement has limited funding, training in evolving scams, and manpower.

Why do scammers scam?

The scammer's goal is money – "it's all about the Benjamins!" They just employ different schemes for the same purpose. To them, it's just business.

Consumers legitimately provide their personal information to banks, retailers, social media platforms, email companies, and every level of government. There's a market for consumer data – much of it is sold, some of it is stolen.

Data that's sold is supposed to be disclosed to us in each company's privacy policy, however many don't read it or follow opt-out offerings. Stolen data we hear about when we're told, or on the news. In those instances we can only secure our accounts with stronger logins.

Scams continue to evolve, often faster than regulations and consumer protection laws can be crafted to control and enforce. Data breaches are now commonplace – and why we must keep login and password information strong and protected.

How do scammers play on our emotions?

The reason scammers succeed is because of the tactics they use – they deceitfully play into our emotions through social engineering, and they don't play fair. In other words, they know it's easy to confuse and try to take advantage of our normal human feelings of:

- Wanting to be helpful,
- Not wanting to appear rude,
- Not wanting to seem confused or dumb, and
- Not wanting to miss an opportunity for something that may be beneficial.

Scammers often disguise themselves behind organizations and brands we already trust and have loyalty to – they call pretending to be them, or send us an email designed with their name & logo but fool us by including scam links they encourage us to click.

This is where we can recognize and outsmart them by engaging our common sense – by being observant, and by asking ourselves critical questions so we can assess what's **real** and **reasonable**.

We can do this now to plan ahead, and we can also do it in the moment.

in THE
coming
pages
you WILL
Learn ...

A STRONG FOUNDATION

01 HOW TO IDENTIFY COMMON SCAM TACTICS

You'll learn how to spot common scam tactics by recognizing red flags like urgent language, suspicious links, impersonation of trusted sources, and requests for sensitive information.

02 RED FLAGS THAT INDICATE POTENTIAL FRAUD

You'll learn to recognize red flags that signal potential fraud, such as unsolicited requests for payment, pressure to act quickly, vague or inconsistent details, and communication from unfamiliar or spoofed sources.

03 STEPS TO PROTECT YOUR PERSONAL INFORMATION

You'll learn how to protect your personal information by using strong passwords, enabling multi-factor authentication, avoiding public Wi-Fi for sensitive tasks, and being cautious about what you share online or respond to via text.

04 WHAT TO DO IF YOU'VE BEEN TARGETED

You'll learn what steps to take if you've been targeted by a scam, including how to report the incident, secure your accounts, monitor for identity theft, and minimize potential financial or personal damage.

05 HOW TO REPORT AND RECOVER FROM SCAMS & FRAUD

You'll learn how to recover from fraud by securing compromised accounts, monitoring your credit, and taking steps to prevent further damage, as well as how to report the incident to the appropriate authorities, financial institutions, and consumer protection agencies to help stop future scams.

06 HOW TO BUILD SKILLS & CONFIDENCE THROUGH KNOWLEDGE

You'll learn how to build skills, confidence and knowledge by understanding how scams work, practicing smart decision-making, and applying proven strategies that empower you to navigate digital threats with clarity and control.

SOME *clarity*

BY THE NUMBERS*

$12B   Lost to fraud in 2024

+25%   Increase from previous year

* Federal Trade Commission

UNDERSTANDING THE DIFFERENCE

"**Security** generally refers to protecting against someone trying to access your stuff — such as stealing your credit card number or hacking your accounts.

Privacy is more often used to talk about keeping your movements from being tracked for purposes of advertising or surveillance."

- Eva Galperin, Electronic Frontier Foundation

SCAM MIX & MATCH

Scams can be perpetuated on any platform— calls, mail, texts, e-mails, social media, package delivery, and in person.

CASCADE

Know that scams and schemes
can cross over and overlap from
one method and platform to
others. The scams you see in
e-mail can also be facilitated by
text messages, phone calls,
social media direct messages
and postal mail. Being hacked
can cause a cascade of issues.

COME FROM A PLACE OF 'NO'

"No" could also be communicated as:

- Not answering a call or responding
- "I'm sorry but I'm not interested."
- Hanging up the call with no words
- Not responding to email and texts

It's okay to say no – don't feel badly or guilty about it! We are not obligated to a caller who could be lying or scamming us. The longer we listen to a scammer, the more they'll think they can talk us into something. The less sure or scared we sound, the more they'll call back to try again.

Our primary goal every day is to protect our security and that of our family – always act in those interests.

Remember that if you're hacked, all your email and phone contacts become vulnerable to becoming the next targets. One hack starts a cascade of others.

Doubt means don't – if our gut feeling or intuition gives us doubt, stop there.

Remember, **if what they say *sounds* too good to be true, it usually *is***.

Even if we aren't sure the caller is legitimate, **we have every right to decline and/or end the call** and to ignore email and texts. Every company, bank and doctor's office is aware of increasing scams. They understand! Legitimate callers attempting to reach you likely have other means of contact.

NOPE,
not today

For the safety of myself, my family, friends, neighbors, and all the contacts in my phone, email, and social media –

I commit to...

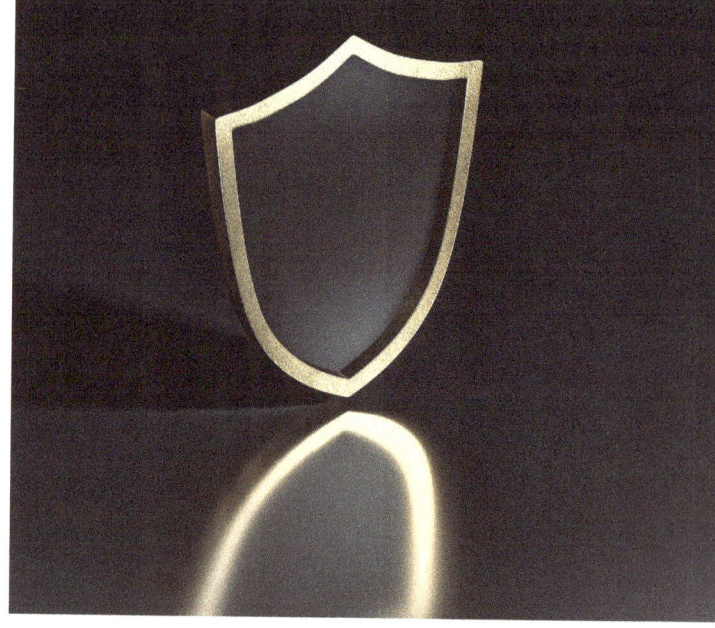

- Not answering calls I don't recognize and let them go to voicemail to assess later.
- Ending any call from someone I don't know – even if it's by hanging up.
- Ignoring and not responding to email and text messages from unknown senders – delete and report as junk/spam.
- Not clicking any links in any message I receive unless I know and trust the sender – and if the message or link appears suspicious, to consider the sender's phone, email, or social media could've been hacked.
- Noticing anything uncharacteristic of a trusted sender & consider they may have been hacked.

I will remember:
- Doubt means don't.
- If it feels off, I'll trust my instincts to be on the safe side.
- If I don't completely understand it and can't easily verify it, I'll treat it as a scam attempt.
- My money and personal data are mine, so I must act to protect it.
- If I'm hacked, other family and friends who are email & text contacts are likely next.
- If I'm not sure or if I get confused, I'll ask someone trusted for their opinion.

BELIEVE *you* CAN & *you* ARE HALFWAY THERE

chapter
02

CHAPTER 02

BIG DATA: BIG BUSINESS

Big data describes vast, fast-moving, and diverse sets of information that traditional tools can't easily manage, requiring advanced computer analytics to uncover patterns and insights.

MASSIVE VOLUME

Platforms like Facebook generate over 4 petabytes of data daily, showcasing the staggering amount of information created every second.

HIGH VELOCITY

Big data moves fast—Twitter users sent around 500 million tweets per day, contributing to the constant stream of real-time data.

BUSINESS VALUE

Companies that effectively use big data can boost their operating margins by up to 60%, thanks to smarter decision-making and predictive insights.

THE SCOPE
OF DATA

Our personal data is extremely valuable. Selling – and stealing – data is big business and most don't realize the scope of it. We often wish we hadn't given our personal information away so easily and assume we made the mistake, but in reality, our data was collected from a mix of volunteered, observed, shared, and inferred sources. Once collected, it's changed hands hundreds of times between brokers, marketers and partners.

Our data is constantly being harvested and traded across digital platforms, often without our knowledge or control. This unchecked flow of personal information has left us exposed to exploitation, manipulation, and breaches that can ripple through every part of our lives.

THE SOURCES OF OUR DATA

Companies, especially brokers, collect personal data from many pipelines:

VOLUNTARILY, BY US

- Forms & sign-ups – think rewards programs, theme park wristbands, warranty cards, or service registrations
- Surveys & quizzes – online quizzes and even some job applications
- Contests & giveaways – entries often exchange contact info for marketing use

Scammers can use their own computer programs and data analytics with social media quizzes to attempt to crack passwords.

SENSORS & DEVICES (EMERGING)

- Location Tracking - phones, GPS in cars, wearable devices (fitness trackers), toll passes
- Smart Home Tech - doorbell cameras, voice assistants (like Google & Alexa), and thermostats collect behavioral data
- IoT Devices – everything from smart fridges to connected TVs feed companies usage data

With security cameras, doorbell cameras, and all smart products with wifi connectivity be sure to change the default password during setup or anyone can access it.

INFERRED OR PREDICTED DATA

Even if you never tell them directly, algorithms infer - age, income, marital status, health conditions, interests, and political leanings from our purchases.

OUR OFFLINE TRANSACTIONS

- Retail Purchases - store loyalty cards (grocery, pharmacy, big box) track your buying habits.
- Public Records - property ownership, voter registration, marriage licenses, and court filings are public and scraped by brokers
- Utilities & Subscriptions - cable, internet, and magazine subscriptions sometimes share or sell data

THIRD PARTIES (WHO BOUGHT & SOLD)

- Credit Bureaus - sell marketing lists (not your full credit report, but predictive scores or segments)
- Data Brokers - aggregate from many sources, then resell packaged profiles
- Business Partnerships - companies often swap customer lists with "partners"

OUR ONLINE ACTIVITY

- Browsing History & Cookies - websites track what pages we visit, what we click, and for how long
- Mobile Apps - often request access to contacts, location, microphone, or photos (sometimes unnecessarily)
- Search Engines & Social Media – every search, like, or share becomes part of our profiles.
- Online Purchases - what we buy (size, color, time of day, how long it took you to make the purchase), how often, and payment methods are recorded and resold

OUR CREDIT, AND HOW TO PROTECT IT

FREE ANNUAL CREDIT REPORT

Exercise your option for free annual credit reports for *every member of your family* regardless of age; the more secure you are, the more secure your family is.

CREDIT FREEZE

Not to be confused with credit monitoring, a credit freeze – aka credit report freeze, credit report lockdown, credit lock, and security freeze – allows consumers to control how a credit reporting agency is allowed to sell their personal data.

A credit freeze locks down the consumer's data, allowing the consumer to give or withhold permission for release. A freeze does not impact the consumer's current accounts or credit score, and there is no cost associated with exercising this option.

If a consumer has instituted a credit freeze, no credit will be extended to the consumer or the identity thief until permission is granted by the consumer (in advance or in response to the credit request).

Pro tip: If you opt for a credit freeze, establish an account at each bureau online you can pause for last-minute furniture or car shopping, otherwise you may experience delay with financing.

SOCIAL MEDIA PRIVACY SETTINGS

Social media platforms are always evolving and pushing updates; some of these revert previously-selected privacy settings to disengage – it's not a one-&-done.

Privacy settings allow you some control over how platforms handle and display your content on their site/app. Consider opting out of ad personalization and access to camera and photos. Privacy settings vary by platform and require user attention – it's up to you to guard your privacy.

CONSIDERATIONS

- Go to each platform's settings to review and update privacy options
- Engage two-factor authentication (2FA) to prevent account takeover
- Don't assume you don't have an account; one could have been impersonated using photos from your real accounts or from your family member's unprotected accounts
- Establish a practice of conducting quarterly or semi-annual online footprint checks for yourself and your family members. Things are always changing. Google yourself and your kids so you know what's public – knowledge is power!
- Build good security habits for the kids in your family, it will serve them well

---

if you aren't paying for the product, you are the product

WHO'S GOT MY DATA?

The short answer is you should assume your data has been sold over and over again and likely also stolen in the numerous breaches that have occurred over the past decade. This is exactly why contact through mail, social media, and digital communications should be met with some degree of skepticism and caution.

While the number of data brokers numbers into the thousands, there are six to ten major brokers that control much of the data broker economy. You can opt out and request your data not be sold.

WHY DO THEY NEED MY DATA?

Most every business uses data analytics to know the exact response, amount of time, number of clicks and comments, and many more metrics to hone their campaigns and get the edge on production decisions and competition. This means they need data for computer programs and artificial intelligence analysis. Because consumers and markets are always evolving, stale data must be routinely replaced with current data.

Examples include insurance companies using your insured vehicle data and even drone footage of your insured property to assess risk and make renewal and pricing decisions. 2024 brought grocery stores implementing digital shelf pricing, bringing consumer concerns of the potential for fluctuating pricing during "peak" times of the day.

Data analytics is used to focus on providing insights into people's actions. Behavioral analytics is used in e-commerce, gaming, social media, and other applications to identify optimization opportunities to realize specific business outcomes. Think grocery and pharmacy shopping cards we scan, and theme park bracelets.

OPT-OUT RESOURCES

Start with the major credit reporting agencies; they are required by law (in the U.S.) to allow consumers to opt out of pre-screened offers. Follow that up with the major data brokers, then marketing and ad tracking.

Opt-Out List	*Resources**
CREDIT REPORTING AGENCIES	• Equifax: *https://www.optoutprescreen.com/* • Experian: *https://www.optoutprescreen.com/* • TransUnion: *https://www.optoutprescreen.com/* • Innovis: *https://www.innovis.com/personal/optout/* *Submit online request or call toll-free numbers. Allow 5-10 business days for confirmation.*
MAJOR DATA BROKERS	• LexisNexis: *https://optout.lexisnexis.com* • Acxiom: *https://www.optoutprescreen.com/* • Spokeo: *https://www.spokeo.com/optout* • Intelius: *https://www.intelius.com/opt-out* • Whitepages: *https://www.whitepages.com/suppression_requests* • MyLife: *https://www.mylife.com/ccpa/opt-out* • PeopleFinder: *https://www.peoplefinder.com/manage* *Follow instructions to remove your listing or request suppression.*
MARKETING & AD TRACKING	• Direct Mail & Pre-Screened Offers: *https://www.optoutprescreen.com/* • Email Marketing: *Use unsubscribe links in emails* • Google: *https://adssettings.google.com/* • Facebook/Meta: *https://www.facebook.com/settings/adpreferences* • Mobile Devices: *Enable 'Limit Ad Tracking' in iOS or 'Opt out of Ads Personalization' in Android.*

Opt-Out List	Resources*
PEOPLE SEARCH & PUBLIC RECORDS SITES	• Search your name on people search engines (e.g., Pipl, BeenVerified, PeekYou) • Follow opt-out procedures (web form or email request)
OPT-OUT RECORD & RECORD MONITORING	• Maintain a spreadsheet of sites contacted, date of request, and confirmation. • Recheck quarterly. • Consider automated services like DeleteMe or OneRep for ongoing monitoring
BONUT TIPS FOR EXTRA PRIVACY	• Use a separate email for marketing and account sign-ups • Limit sharing of personal info on social media • Regularly clear cookies and browser history or use privacy-focused browsers/extensions
FREE ANNUAL CREDIT REPORT	Exercise your option for free annual credit reports for **every member** of your family regardless of age; the more secure you are, the more secure your family is.

Use Privacy Laws to Your Advantage
- California Residents: CCPA lets you request deletion of personal data.
- Other states: Nevada, Virginia, Colorado, etc. have similar laws.
- Action: Contact companies to request opt-out under these laws.

Links may change; search for company + "opt out" and follow prompts

FREEZE RESOURCES

Our data is stored and used in a myriad of places, and it should come as no shock that credit reporting bureaus own other reporting and data companies. By creating an account with each, you can freeze and unfreeze your credit file as needed. Anyone needing assistance from consumer support can call using the phone numbers listed on the site (not from Google or other search engine).

Reminder: Be sure to unfreeze these prior to applying for financing to avoid confusion and delay.

Freeze List	Resources*
CREDIT REPORTING AGENCIES	<ul><li>Equifax: *https://www.equifax.com/personal/credit-report-services/*</li><li>Experian: *https://www.experian.com/help/credit-freeze/*</li><li>TransUnion: *https://www.transunion.com/credit-advice*</li><li>Innovis: *https://www.innovis.com/personal/securityfreeze*</li><li>Clarity Services: *https://www.clarityservices.com/support/security-freeze/*</li><li>DataX: *https://consumers.dataxltd.com/consumerCreditFreeze*</li><li>FactorTrust: *https://www.factortrust.com/Consumer/CreditFreeze/Landing.aspx*</li></ul>
BANK ACCOUNT SECURITY	To block banks and credit unions from accessing account history without permission and to prevent identity theft and unauthorized account opening: <ul><li>ChexSystems: *https://www.chexsystems.com/security-freeze/place-freeze*</li></ul>
UTILITY SECURITY	To prevent telecom, utility, and pay TV companies from accessing account history without your permission, and to help protect against identity theft and unauthorized service applications: <ul><li>National Consumer Telecom & Utilities Exchange (NCTUE): *https://nctue.com/consumer/*</li></ul>

* Links may change; search for company + "freeze" and follow prompts to official websites

CHAPTER

03

PHONE & TEXT SCAMS

Phone and text scams are designed to trick people into giving away personal information, money, or access to their accounts. Scammers often impersonate trusted institutions like banks, delivery services, or government agencies to create urgency and fear. These scams can include fake prize notifications, fraudulent account alerts, or requests for payment via gift cards or wire transfers. Many victims are caught off guard because the messages appear convincing and are timed to feel relevant. Staying alert, verifying sources, and never clicking suspicious links are key to protecting yourself from these increasingly sophisticated attacks.

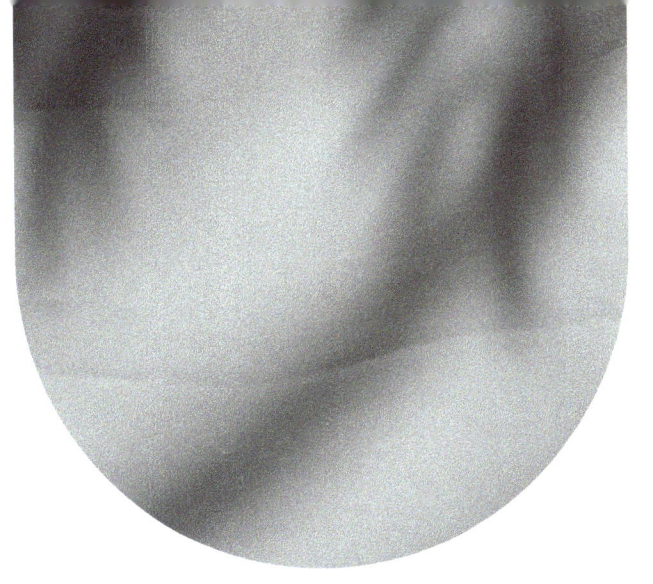

PHONE & TEXT COMMON SCAM METHODS

KNOW WHO YOU'RE ENGAGING WITH

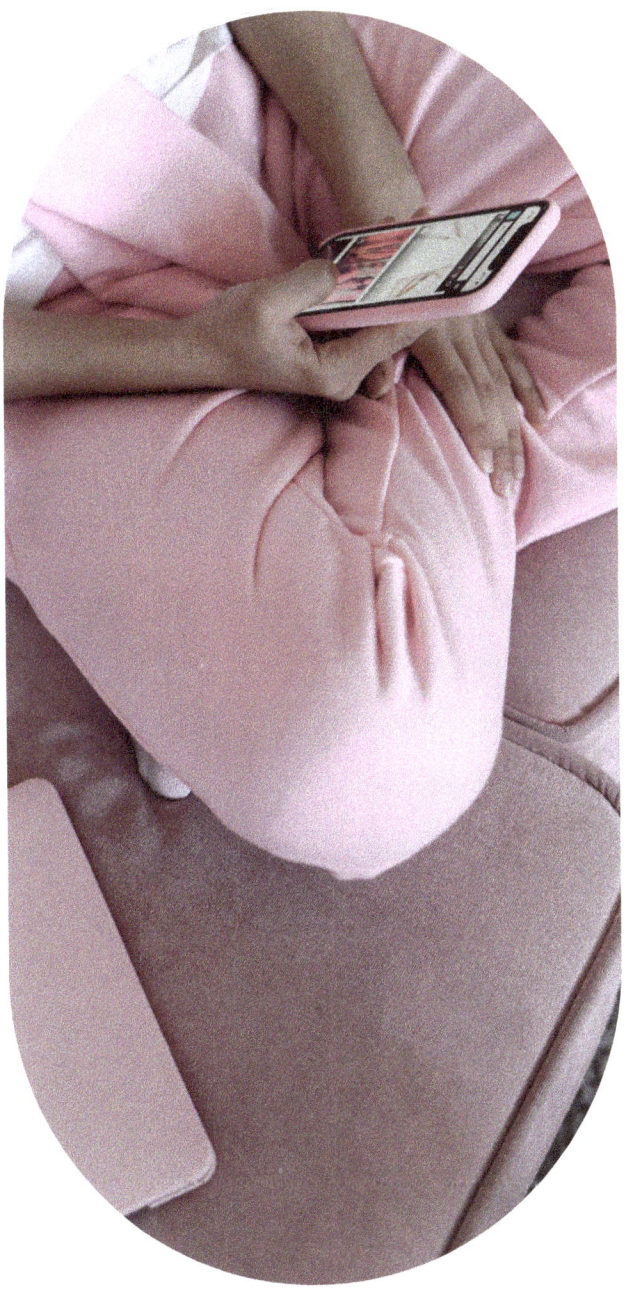

COMMON TEXT SCAMS
FAKE PACKAGE DELIVERY
FAKE SECURITY ALERT
FAKE PUCHASE CONFIRMATION
PRIZE NOTIFICATION
CHARITY/FOUNDATION DONATION REQUEST
POLITICAL CAMPAIGN MESSAGES

Phone scammers use sophisticated tactics to look and sound legitimate, sometimes creating urgency for you to feel pressured for time. They often spoof others' phone numbers to control the number appearing in your Caller ID – maybe a trusted person's number. They also often impersonate government agencies, banks, or tech companies.

Spoofing – pretending to be something or someone else to mislead.(Example: fake caller ID, forged email address, or imitated website).

Smishing – pretending to be a trusted source (bank, delivery service, government agency) to trick you into clicking a malicious link or attachment, downloading malware through a scheme, or giving up passwords, Social Security number, or credit card details.

HIGH VULNERABILITY: GEN Z (18-39)

Younger adults aged 18–39 are the most vulnerable to text scams because they engage heavily with digital platforms, trust online interactions, and are frequently targeted with scams tailored to their habits. They're most vulnerable to online shopping, job offers and crypto scams.

HIGH VULNERABILITY: MILLENNIAL (25-39)

Millennials are especially vulnerable to text scams because their constant digital engagement and trust in social media and online services make them prime targets for fake investment offers, service frauds, and phishing schemes.

MODERATE VULNERABILITY: GEN-X (40-59)

Gen X is moderately vulnerable to text scams because they're active online but often targeted with more sophisticated phishing and impersonation tactics that exploit their professional responsibilities and trust in familiar institutions. They're also more vulnerable to romance scams.

MODERATE VULNERABILITY: SENIORS (60+)

Adults aged 60 and over are less frequently targeted by text scams but tend to suffer higher financial losses when they are, often due to scams exploiting trust in authority figures or unfamiliarity with newer technology.

Text message scams are projected to cost Americans between $15–18 billion in 2025; there are estimated >95 billion spam texts sent annually.

Text Scam EXAMPLES

TRANSACTION APPROVAL SCAM

+63 950 ▬▬▬

Unverified Apple Pay Usage,

We noticed some unusual activity on your Apple ID (Case ID: 64918273508) account and want to ensure your information remains safe.

Details of the activity:

Transaction: $215.45 at "Electronic Hub USA"

Date/Time: August 29, 2025, at 10:47 AM (PST)

Device: iPhone 14 Pro, used in San Diego, CA

If you recognize this transaction, no action is needed.

If this activity is familiar, no action is required, and the transaction will proceed within 24 hours. If not, contact Apple Support immediately at +1-805-▬▬▬ for assistance.

Need ▬▬▬▬▬?

Apple Support: +1-805-▬▬▬ Billing Help: https://getsupport.apple.com/

Thank you for helping keep your account secure.

Stay secure, Apple Security Division

The sender is not in your contact list.
Report Junk

+ Text Message · SMS

01 SENDER NUMBER + COUNTRY CODE

The sender – "+63" number – is not a country code of the U.S. The U.S. country code is "1." While Apple products may be produced or manufactured at least in part in other countries, Apple is an American company headquartered in the U.S. This is a hallmark red flag for any text message.

02 ATTEMPT TO PROMPT CONTACT

By trying to appear as Apple, this text attempts to gain your engagement through a fake transaction. Contact is not needed or advised to check your Apple account and any wallet credit cards to verify any transaction occurred. If a fraudulent transaction did occur, there are methods in place to dispute it without engagement through text.

03 FAKE CUSTOMER SERVICE

While many know of this scam and would automatically question the legitimacy of this text, a quick search engine check immediately returns references of this being a scam. Apple Security Division, if it exists, does not engage with customers in this way.

LEGAL ACTION SCAM

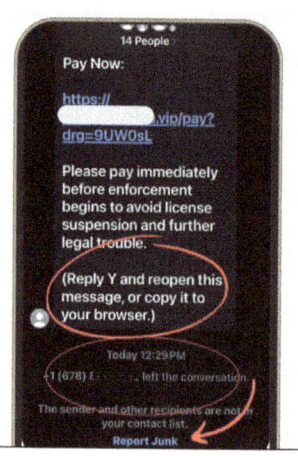

01   RECIPIENT LIST + PHONE NUMBERS

Once again, we are supposed to believe that the Georgia DMV would send a text to me and 13 others without protecting their personal contact information? That violates any state's privacy policy.

02   FALSE + MISLEADING LEGAL REFERENCE

A quick check of this legal reference shows no such code and reference to scammers using this reference in scam texts.

03   URGENCY + FEAR TACTIC USED

Common in these texts is the appearance you're in violation. While the Georgia DMV may provide these consequences on their website or in a printed letter mailed to you, most DMVs simply suspend someone's license and wait for them to make contact once they figure it out or are stopped by police. DMVs aren't known to chase people down.

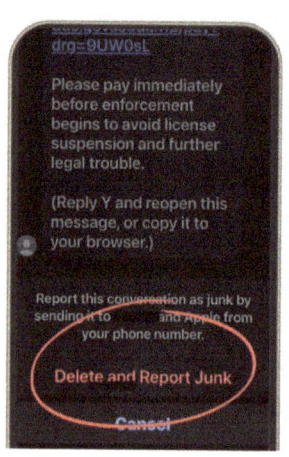

04   CONTACT ATTEMPT

Clicking the link could install malware on your computer or device, making you vulnerable to data theft, account takeovers, device camera or microphone activation, surveillance of activity, theft of passwords, and/or identity theft. Responding "Y" would initiate text or a phone call from the scammer with the same pressures.

PACKAGE DELIVERY TEXT SCAM

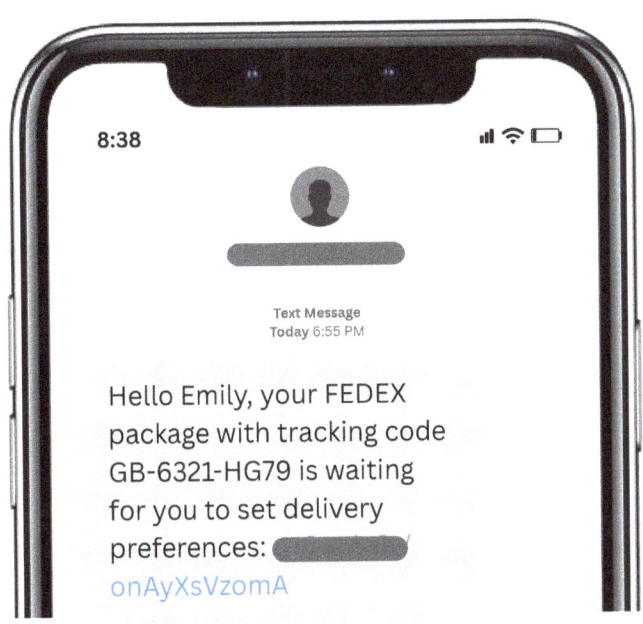

Method: Email or text to make you think it's real & you'll miss out if you don't respond.

Goal: To get you to click the link to install malware on your device or to open communication.

Considerations:
- Would the shipping company have your number?
- Are you expecting a package?
- Ignore the text, even if that inserts delivery delay.

HUMAN ENGAGEMENT SCAM

Method: Scam email or text to make you think it's real & you need to take the action instructed.

Goal: To get you to make contact to (1) confirm the number is active, and (2) to open conversation to facilitate the scam.

Considerations:
- Is it characteristic of your family member to inform you of a new number this way?
- Verify by calling the old number, or by not responding and waiting for them to contact you.

JOB OPPORTUNITY SCAM

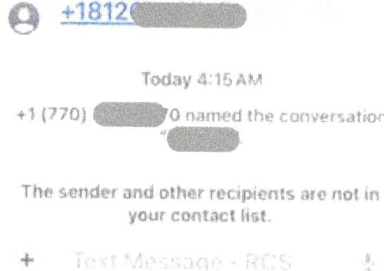

01 SENDER NUMBER + NUMBER CHANGES

The sender – the 212 area code number – is different from the 6-digit code label, which was created by the 770 area code number at the bottom. Sometimes legitimate texts come from a short series of numbers. The sender was attempting to mask this as legitimate.

02 RECIPIENT LIST + PHONE NUMBERS

Legitimate senders generally have privacy policies which protect the information of those doing business with them. Here, you see the contact information of all recipients. This alone makes this text suspicious and deserving of deletion.

03 DOLLAR FIGURES + SALARY INFO

Most legitimate businesses don't advertise salary levels like this. Very suspicious is the format of the figure as "US300" instead of the common way businesses in the US format figures as "$300." This should lead the recipient to question if the sender is in the US. This sender, though on the surface appears to be using a domestic phone number and in the US, likely spoofed a legitimate person's phone number from purchased or stolen data and used it, while its actual U.S. owner is unaware.

"WHAT IF THIS IS REAL?"

These are common text scams meant to make you think you've already been hacked. If you respond, you put yourself at risk of trouble. If you have an account with that platform, you'll know if it's real when you verify the status by logging in elsewhere.

Again: DELETE > REPORT JUNK

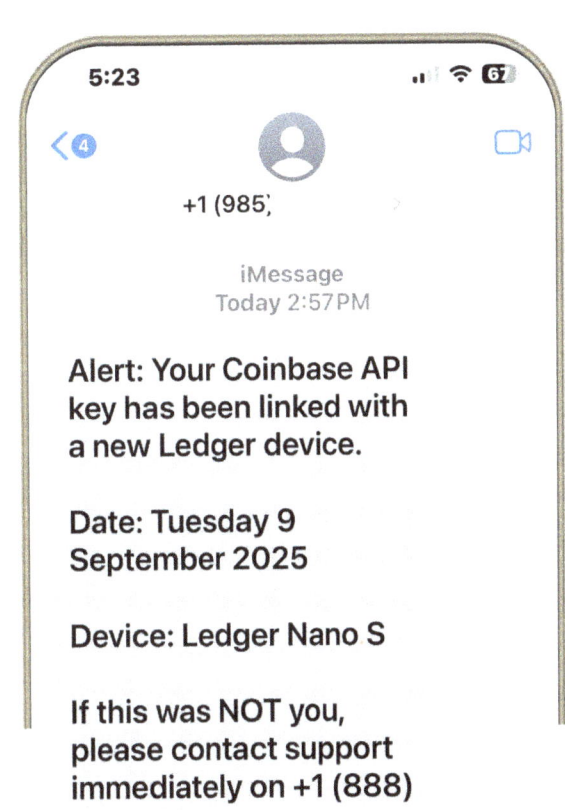

5:23

+1 (985)

iMessage
Today 2:57 PM

Alert: Your Coinbase API key has been linked with a new Ledger device.

Date: Tuesday 9 September 2025

Device: Ledger Nano S

If this was NOT you, please contact support immediately on +1 (888) 3(

Another day, another peppering of messages...

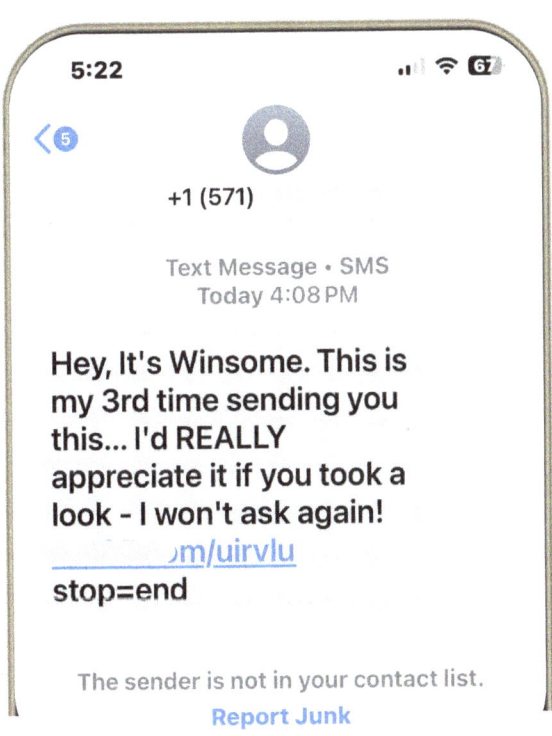

5:22

+1 (571)

Text Message • SMS
Today 4:08 PM

Hey, It's Winsome. This is my 3rd time sending you this... I'd REALLY appreciate it if you took a look - I won't ask again!
)m/uirvlu
stop=end

The sender is not in your contact list.
Report Junk

"I DON'T WANT TO BE RUDE"

While you could've forgotten to record an acquaintance's phone number in your phone, it's far more likely this is a scam attempting to get you to click the link or respond in any way to verify the number is active.

DELETE > REPORT JUNK

Any other action puts you at risk of being hacked.

"UGH... POLITICS..."

Love politics – or love to hate it – hackers know some are passionate for or against political parties and their actions. The truth is, this text is from a hacker likely having nothing to do with politics. Whatever you do, don't respond.

DELETE and REPORT JUNK

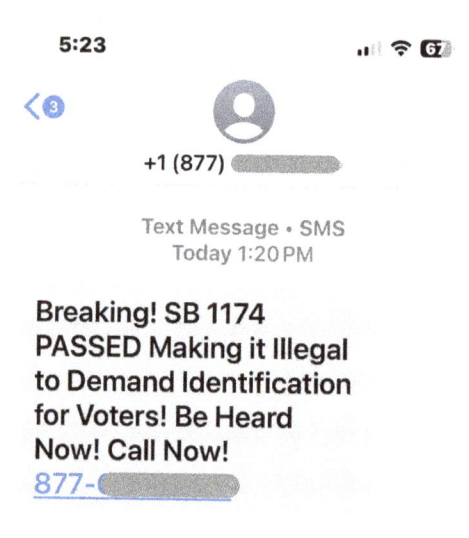

DELETE > REPORT JUNK

You can simply delete the message, and you can click "Report Junk," but the fastest way to accomplish both is:

DELETE and REPORT JUNK

Pro tip: You can usually slide the message from the main list and Delete and Report Junk directly from that list.

SILENCE –

it's the best response

Phone Number SPOOFING PROTECTION

THE TRUTH IN CALLER ID ACT (2009)

(47 U.S.C. § 227(e)) made spoofing with illegal intent illegal. With (1) many spammers overseas and out of US jurisdiction, (2) law enforcement staffing and training unstaffed to devote necessary manpower to investigate, and (3) scammers' successful use of anonymity tactics, it's a challenge to enforce federal law with every victim.

FCC'S STIR/SHAKEN MANDATE (2019)

Using its authority under the Truth in Caller ID Act and the TRACED Act, the FCC required major voice service providers to implement STIR/SHAKEN caller ID authentication in the IP portions of their networks. This tech verifies that a call is actually coming from the number displayed, helping block or label spoofed calls.

THE TRACED ACT (2019)

(Pub. L. 116-105), Telephone Robocall Abuse Criminal Enforcement and Deterrence:
- Directed the FCC to require providers to implement caller ID authentication (STIR/SHAKEN).
- Expanded penalties for illegal robocalls and spoofing.
- Required the FCC to ensure even smaller and rural carriers adopt anti-spoofing protections.

PROTECTION STRATEGIES

1. **Log into your mobile company account.** The STIR/SHAKEN mandate requires service providers to provide protections, but you need to activate them.
2. **Never give personal information to unsolicited callers**. Hang up and call the organization directly using a number you find independently, not one provided by the caller or found on a search engine.

CHAPTER
04

E-MAIL SCAMS

Email scams are deceptive messages designed to trick recipients into revealing sensitive information, sending money, or downloading malicious software. These scams often masquerade as legitimate communications from trusted sources—like banks, government agencies, or well-known companies—and use tactics such as urgent language, fake invoices, or enticing offers to lure victims. Common types include phishing, where scammers steal login credentials; malware distribution through infected attachments; and email compromise, which targets corporate accounts for financial fraud. With scammers constantly evolving their techniques, staying alert to red flags—like generic greetings, suspicious links, and unexpected requests—is essential to protecting your personal and financial data.

E-MAIL & PHISHING

Phishing emails are deceptive messages designed to trick the recipients into revealing sensitive information often by impersonating trusted sources like banks, coworkers, or popular services. They use your personal data (purchased or stolen) to sound legitimate.

"PHISHING"

Email remains a common form for digital scams. Phishing emails are designed to steal your personal information, passwords, or money. Scammers send attempts far and wide, "casting a net." Statistically, they "catch" victims.

Phishing is a play on words describing a fishing metaphor:

RED FLAGS

- ☐ Urgent language: "Act now!" "Limited time!" "Immediate action required."
- ☐ Generic Greetings: "Dear Customer" instead of your name
- ☐ Suspicious sender address not matching organization
- ☐ Poor grammar and spelling errors
- ☐ Requests for sensitive information via mail
- ☐ Threatening consequences for not acting immediately

PASSWORD
OR PERSONAL DATA

FISHING
CASTING A LURE & HOPING SOMEONE BITES

How to Verify E-mail Legitimacy

- Check the sender's email address carefully
- Hover over links without clicking to see the real destination
- Contact the organization directly using official contact information
- Look for official logos and branding inconsistencies
- Be suspicious of unexpected attachments

Never Click If...

The email asks you to verify account information, update payment details, or claims your account will be closed. Legitimate companies don't request sensitive information via email.

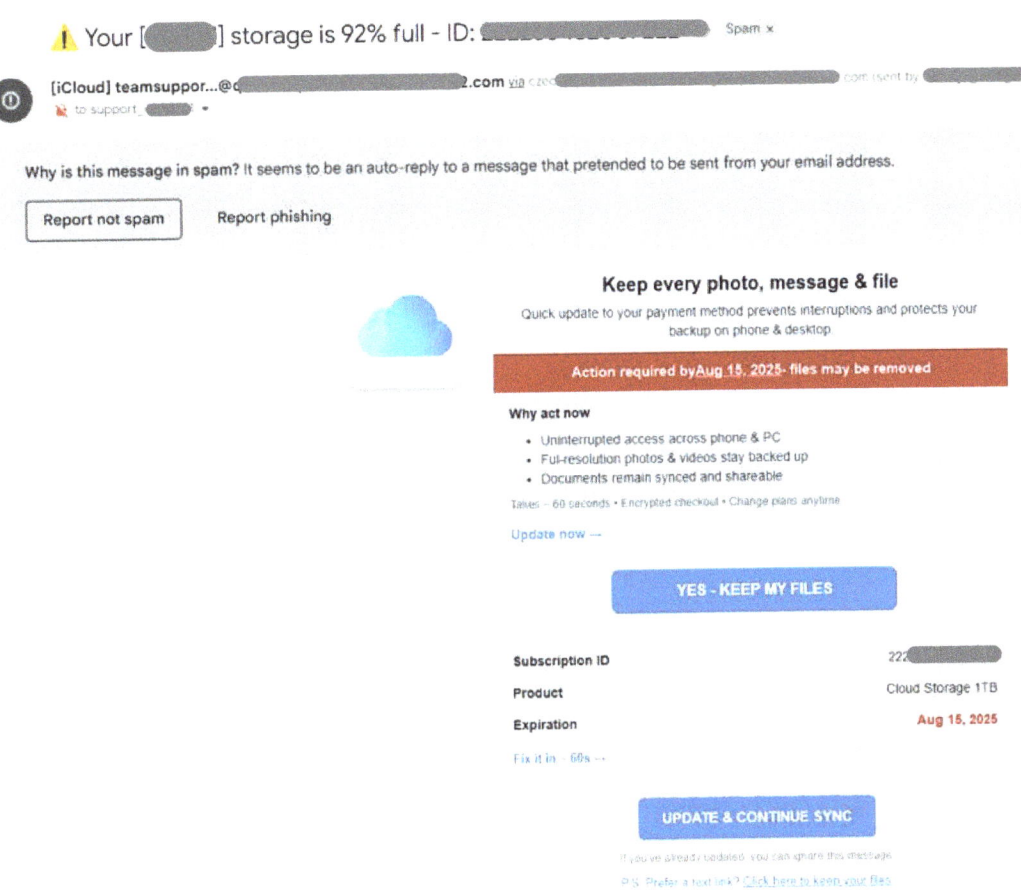

TRANSACTION APPROVAL SCAM

METHOD

Email or text to make you think you owe money or are past due.

GOAL

To get you to click the link to install malware on your device, or open communication.

RED FLAGS

- Sender address doesn't look right
- Do I even have a cloud storage backup plan for my data?

If so, I can verify through other means without clicking or responding to this email.

THE SKEPTICAL MINDSET

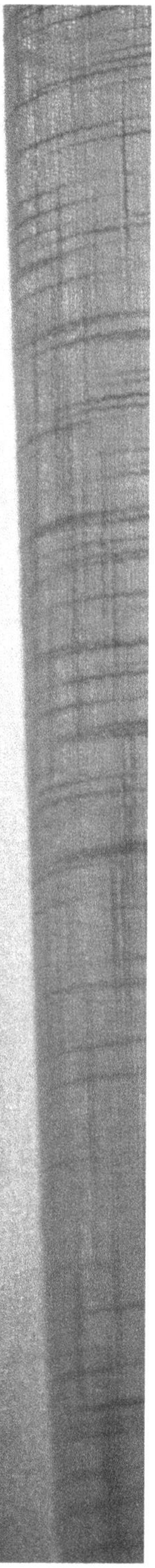

DO NOT:

☐ **Don't click suspicious links**
Hover first to preview the URL; if it looks odd or mismatched, skip it.

☐ **Don't download unexpected attachments**
They could contain malware or ransomware

☐ **Don't trust urgent or threatening messages**
Scammers use fear to rush your judgment

☐ **Don't share personal info via e-mail**
Legitimate companies wouldn't ask for sensitive data this way

☐ **Don't reply to unknown senders**
It confirms your e-mail is active and invites additional spam

☐ **Don't assume logos & look mean legitimacy**
Scammers often copy branding to look official & convincing

☐ **Don't ignore spelling & grammar errors**
These are classic signs of phishing attempts

☐ **Don't use/reuse passwords across accounts**
If one gets compromised, others are at risk

☐ **Don't rely solely on spam filters**
They help, but scammers constantly evolve their tactics

Approaching e-mail with a skeptical mindset isn't overreacting – it's being smart.

doubt

means

don't

e-mail
"FLOOD"

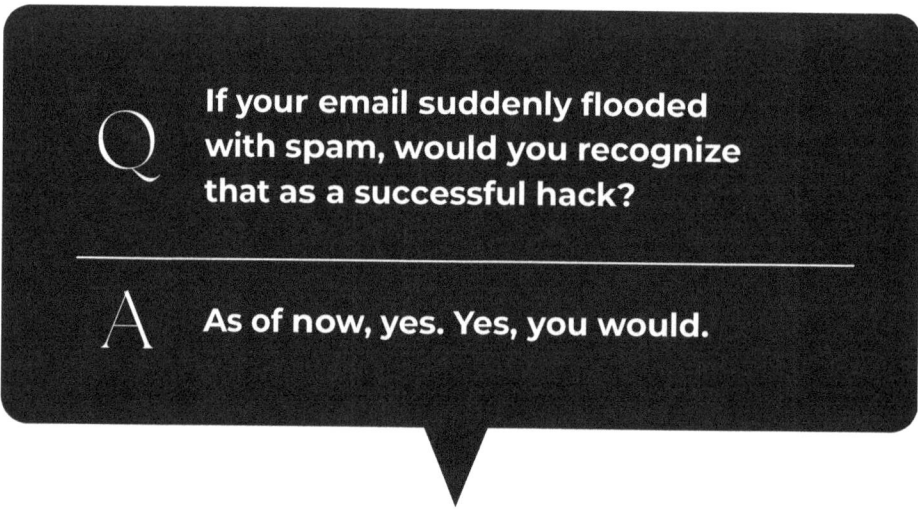

Q If your email suddenly flooded with spam, would you recognize that as a successful hack?

A As of now, yes. Yes, you would.

If you notice your inbox suddenly being overwhelmed with spam, it's a sign that a scammer is actively hacking one of your accounts.

This tactic, sometimes called an email bomb, blast, or flood, is designed to bury your real messages so you overlook an important email — often one containing a security code used for Two-Factor Authentication (2FA) or Multi-Factor Authentication (MFA).

ACT QUICKLY:

1. Check carefully. Scroll through the spam to find any legitimate emails containing a security code and identify which account is being targeted. Look specifically for password reset emails or 2FA/MFA emails containing the security code you'd expect when logging in. Use your e-mail search function, filtering by your bank/credit names.

2. Check your Sent email. If you find emails you didn't send, especially mass messages or ones with suspicious links, your email account may be the one compromised.

3. Take action immediately:

- Contact the financial institution or company involved, report the attempted breach, and ask for assistance.
- Log in to the account (if possible) and change your password right away.

chapter
05

CHAPTER 05

PHONE CALL SCAMS

Phone scams are deceptive schemes where scammers engage us to start a conversation geared ultimately toward fraud. Identifying legitimate business callers from fraudsters can be challenging.

THEIR GOAL

To gain trust under the guise of legitimate business, campaign or charity work with an ultimate goal of fraudulently gaining money or something of value.

THEIR APPEARANCE

We often initially assess their calls as legitimate because of their Caller ID number – which has been faked or "spoofed."

THEIR CLAIM

Whatever business, cause or campaign they claim to represent is not legitimate and we can identify their comments as untrue if we become fraud wise.

ASSESSING PHONE SCAMS

Telephone scammers impersonate legitimate organizations to trick people into giving away money or personal information. These schemes often rely on urgency, fear, or emotional manipulation to pressure and make victims think they need to act quickly.

Phone scams come in many deceptive forms, each designed to exploit trust or fear. Common types include IRS impersonation scams, where callers threaten legal action over unpaid taxes; tech support scams, claiming your device is infected; and bank fraud calls, warning of suspicious account activity. Others include lottery or prize scams, promising fake winnings; charity scams, especially after disasters; family emergency scams, where someone pretends to be a relative in trouble; and business impersonation scams, targeting employees with fake boss requests. More recent threats include AI-powered voice cloning scams, vishing and smishing attacks (voice and text phishing), and debt collection frauds that use intimidation to extract money.

ASSESS EACH CALL

☐ Is there an unexpected urgency?

☐ Request for payment with gift cards/crypto?

☐ Is the offer or story too good to be true?

☐ Threats of arrest or legal action?

☐ Request for sensitive information?

☐ Was the Caller ID fake or "spoofed?"

☐ Does the caller sound robotic or scripted?

☐ Is there no time to verify?

☐ Was the call unsolicited?

Phone Scam
EXAMPLES

CONTEST SCAMS

Telephone contest scams are fraudulent calls where scammers claim you've won a prize—like cash, vacations, or electronics—in a sweepstakes or lottery you never entered. They often impersonate well-known companies or government agencies to sound legitimate, then demand upfront payments for "taxes," "processing fees," or "customs duties" before you can claim your winnings. These scams may also ask for sensitive personal or financial information, putting victims at risk of identity theft. Despite the excitement they generate, there is no real prize—just a ploy to steal your money or data.

To stay safe, never pay to claim a prize, always verify the legitimacy of any contest independently, and avoid sharing sensitive details over the phone. Be cautious of unsolicited calls and resist pressure tactics—legitimate contests don't rush you or demand private data. Staying skeptical is your best defense against these fraudulent schemes.

TECH SUPPORT SCAMS

Tech support scams are fraudulent calls or pop-ups where scammers pretend to be from reputable companies—like Microsoft or Apple—claiming your device has a virus or security issue. They pressure you to grant remote access, install software, or pay for unnecessary services, often stealing personal data or planting malware once inside your system.

To stay safe, remember: real tech companies don't make unsolicited calls, and legitimate error messages never ask you to call. If in doubt, close the window and contact the company directly through verified channels.

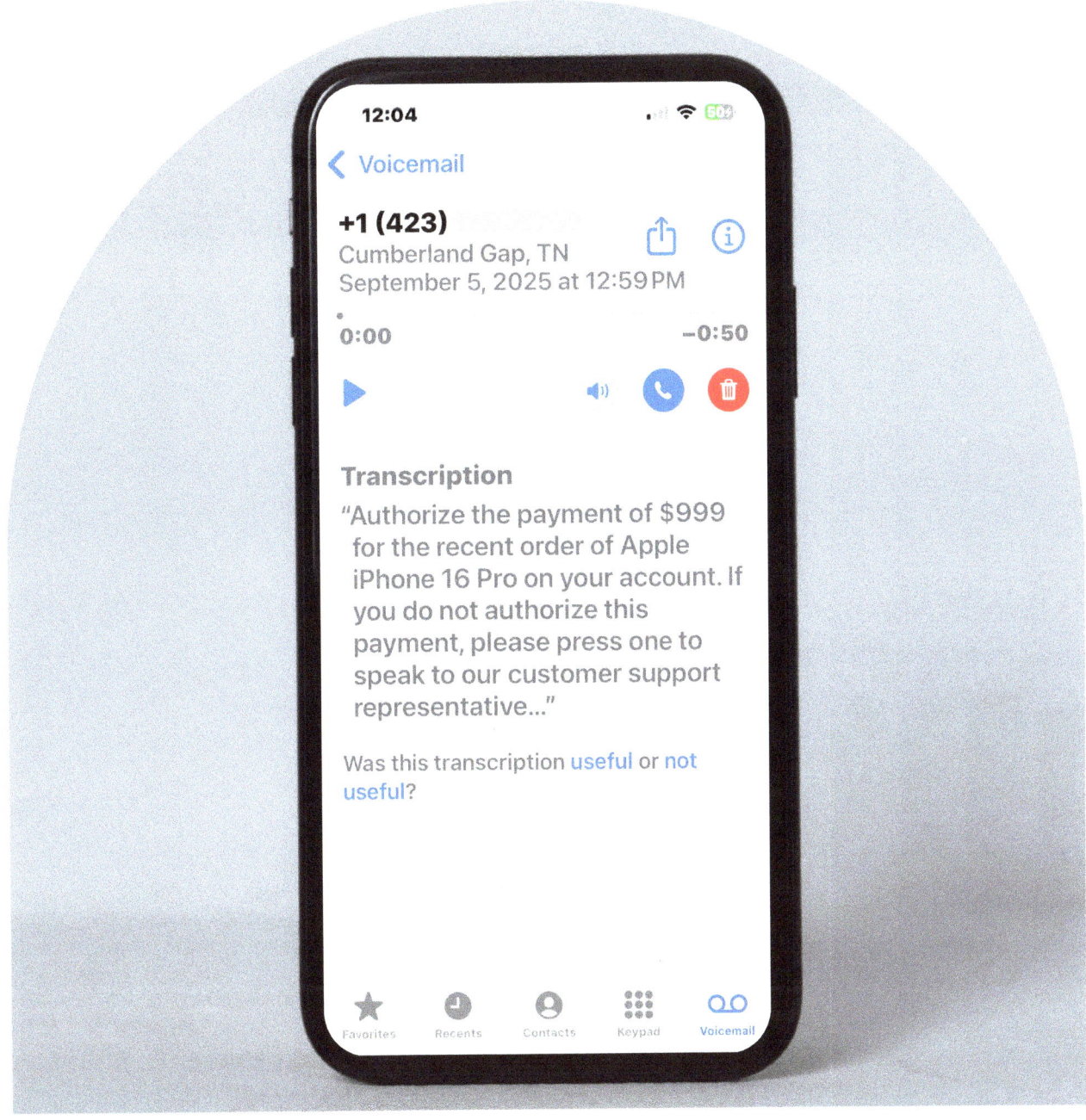

TRANSACTION APPROVAL/CONFIRMATION SCAM

The recipient didn't recognize the number and wisely let the call go to voicemail to assess later. Here, all roads lead to scam. This is a transaction approval/confirmation scam and deserving of ignoring and deletion.

GOVERNMENT IMPERSONATION CALLS

Scammers pretend to be from the IRS, Social Security Administration, or other local/state/federal government agencies, claiming you owe money, or your benefits will be suspended unless you pay immediately.

Important Facts

- Government agencies don't call demanding immediate payment
- Government agencies have established, and reasonable practices usually memorialized in policy available for online review
- They don't ask for payment via gift cards or wire transfers
- Hang up and call the agency directly using official numbers
- Never give personal information over the phone

LAW ENFORCEMENT & COURT OFFICER IMPERSONATION SCAM

One of the most alarming phone scams involves callers impersonating law enforcement officers or court clerks, claiming you've missed jury duty or failed to pay a traffic ticket. These scammers often sound authoritative and may use real names of local officials to boost credibility. They typically say there's a warrant out for your arrest and demand immediate payment to avoid jail time or legal trouble. They may discuss a loved one who is "in custody" and requires immediate bail money. The urgency and fear they create are designed to cloud your judgment, making you more likely to comply without verifying the claims. Payment is usually requested through unconventional methods like gift cards, wire transfers, or cryptocurrency—none of which are used by legitimate government agencies.

These scams are especially dangerous because they often use Caller ID spoofing to make it appear as though the call is coming from a local police department or courthouse. Victims report receiving multiple calls, sometimes with personal details like their full name or address, which adds to the illusion of legitimacy. If you ask for written documentation, scammers may dodge the request or claim it's confidential.

In reality, missing jury duty does not result in arrest warrants issued over the phone, and legitimate summonses are always delivered by mail. Even if a loved one were in custody, arranging bail can take hours or days and any urgency is not on the police or judicial side. If you receive such a call, hang up and contact your local court or law enforcement agency using an official number (not provided by the caller) to verify the claim. If the call is legitimate, the caller would understand.

COMBINATION (PHANTOM HACKER) SCAM

Sophisticated multi-phase fraud where scammers impersonate tech support, financial institutions, and government agencies to convince victims their accounts are transferring their money to fake "safe" accounts, often losing their life savings in the process.

It certainly sounds scary enough. A scheme known as the Phantom Hacker scam actually combines other scams into one sophisticated, multi-phased fraud scheme.

Step 1 – The scam begins with a fake tech support scammer posing as Microsoft, Apple, or "security expert" advising your computer is hacked; they urge you to act quickly and follow their instructions.

Step 2 – You're then "transferred" to a fake bank or government official posing as an FBI agent or employee of the Federal Reserve. This step makes the scheme appear serious and legitimate.

Step 3 – The Money Grab. They warn that hackers are actively hacking your accounts and convince you to move your assets to a so-called safe account (which is actually controlled by the scammers), or to purchase gold, gift cards or cryptocurrency.

Again, pressure to act immediately to protect assets are red flags of this scam. We know that technology companies, banks and the government don't advise customers to transfer money to "safe" accounts.

We also know not to give anyone remote access to our computers unless we are the ones who recognized a concern and initiated contact with a researched and trusted company.

Hanging up the call and contacting our bank directly using a number from the back of your bank card or directly from the bank's website are the best moves.

Artificial INTELLIGENCE

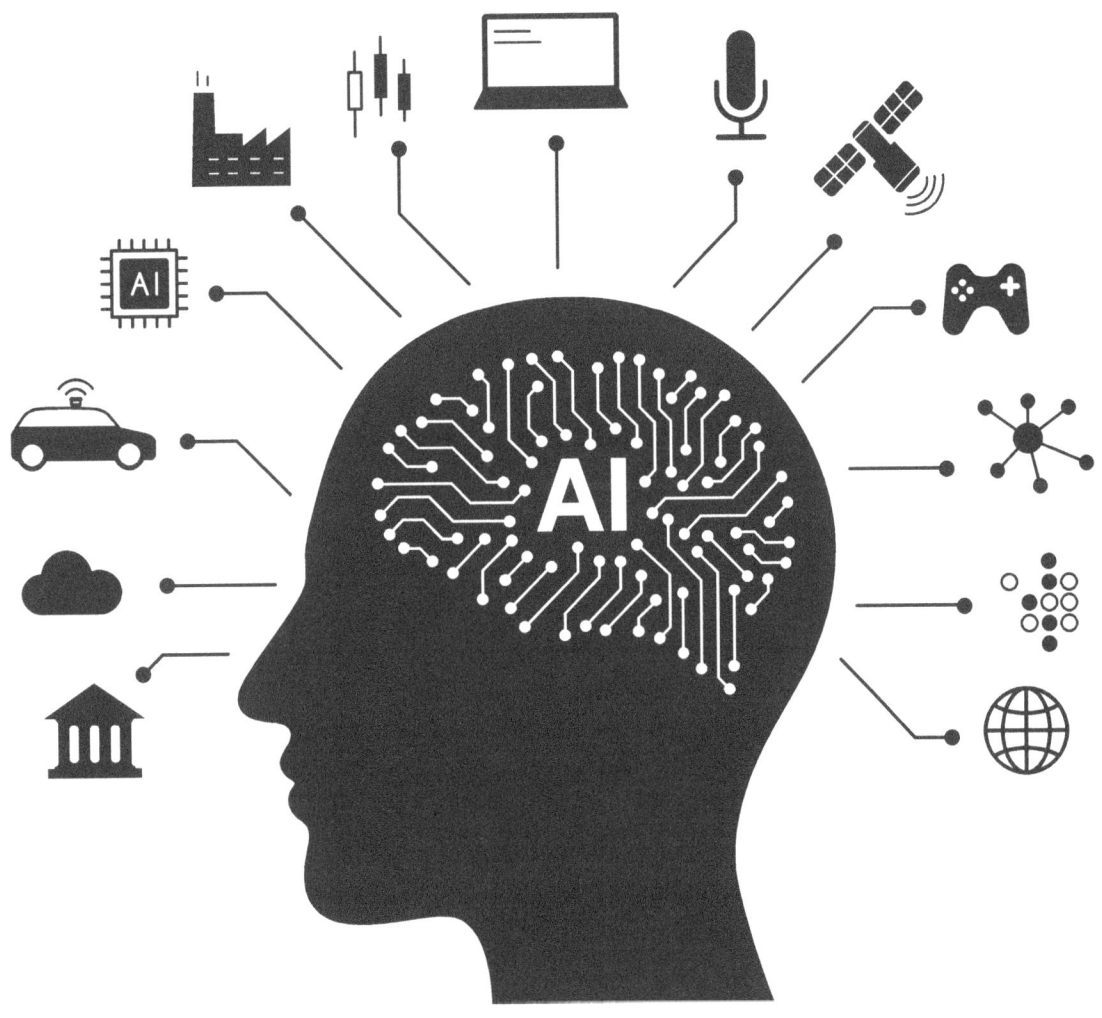

AI and related "deepfake" scams are next-generation fraud schemes. They use synthetic media — digitally altered with AI — to make it appear that someone said or did something they never actually did.

They're referred to as "deepfakes" because they combine a form of AI that uses neural networks, known as "deep learning," with "fake" content that is fabricated or manipulated.

AI programs owned by various companies are processing vast amounts of information from nearly every imaginable source in what is known as machine learning — think encyclopedias, textbooks, recordings, music, retail catalogs, website content, archived records, and more.

Scammers are using and perfecting ways of using AI to create fake voices, videos and images to impersonate people – including relatives and friends. They look and sound authentic. Example: You may see a video that is real paired with audio of the person speaking something they didn't say.

Q. How can we combat this? Be prepared?

A. By discussing it, having a plan, & a family-only password.

*Have you spotted the AI
image in this book?
Look closely at the image on page 14.*

HOW TO HANDLE AI CALLS

The scammer's goal is to confront you with the chaos of an urgency under the guise of a medical emergency, accident, arrest, or kidnapping of someone you care for. The call appears genuine down to the correct phone number in caller ID.

Your first move will be to control your feelings and engage your analytical skills:

If I'm told my loved one is in an accident or experiencing a medical emergency, then they're in a position to receive medical care. What's the urgency? No payment is due immediately.

If I'm told my loved one has been arrested, then they're in the custody of sworn officers. Bail funds are never due immediately and staff know it takes hours or days to arrange bail & release.

If I'm told my loved one has been kidnapped, this is an actual emergency if real. How can we know if it's real? Call that person or other family members and call 911 regardless of what the caller says. Real and fake kidnappers are criminals and can't be trusted. Chances are, your "kidnapped" loved one is fine and is unaware of the ongoing scam.

If the call is coming from my loved one, it could be an AI copy of their voice. Verify by calling them back and call 911. If your family has an established password for emergencies, ask for it.

Scammers spoof phone numbers by falsifying Caller ID information to make us believe we know who's calling.

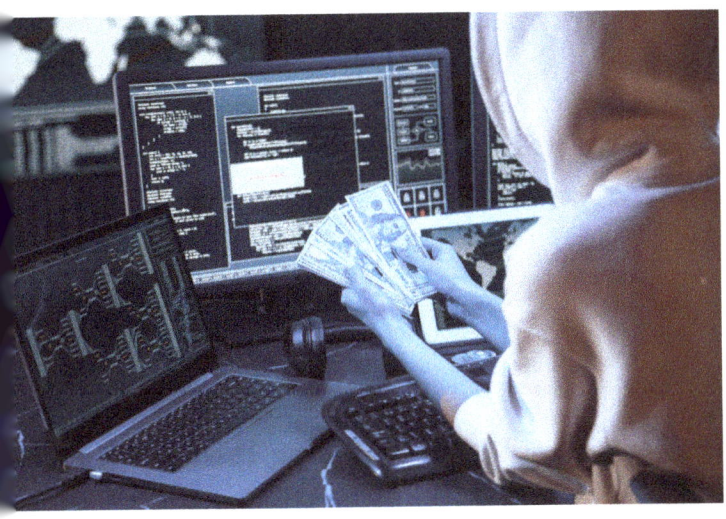

fail to plan, plan to fail.

THE DREADED
unsolicited call

We all receive them, but scammers are getting smarter – we must outsmart them.

Think about and practice how you might handle these callers.

5 Red Flags

These almost always mean you're dealing with a scam:

- They pressure you to act immediately.
- They ask for gift cards, wire transfers, or crypto.
- They want remote access to your computer.
- They say "don't tell anyone."
- They threaten you with arrest or fines.

Best Practices

- Don't answer calls from unknown numbers; let voicemail answer those.
- Hang up immediately if it feels wrong.
- Never give any personal information, even if they share something correct.
- Don't trust Caller ID alone, scammers spoof numbers.
- Use a call-blocker app (many are free).
- Report the call to the Federal Trade Commission at donotcall.gov.

CHAPTER 06

COMMON SCAM METHODS

Scammers use a wide range of deceptive tactics to exploit trust, urgency, and confusion. They use our personal data (bought or stolen) to sound convincing. Common methods include phishing emails that mimic legitimate companies to steal login credentials, imposter scams where fraudsters pose as government officials or tech support, and investment frauds promising high returns with little risk. Others include romance scams, where emotional manipulation leads to financial loss, and subscription bomb attacks, which flood inboxes to hide real alerts. Scammers also exploit disasters through charity fraud, and target older adults with tech support or prize scams. Their strategies evolve constantly, making vigilance and skepticism essential defenses.

ONLINE SHOPPING SCAMS

Fake online stores and e-commerce marketplace scams trick shoppers into paying for products they'll never receive, or receiving counterfeit goods. These sites often have URLs/links that are ever-so-slightly different from the real ones.

Marketplace scammers use legitimate platforms including eBay, Facebook Marketplace, and Craigslist to defraud buyers and sellers. They often promote deals that look too good or discounted to be believed.

✴ SAFE SHOPPING PLAN

- Research the seller's reputation and reviews
- Use secure payment methods with buyer protection
- Verify the website's SSL certificate (https://)
- Check the return and refund policy
- Look up the company's Better Business Bureau rating
- Be wary of deals seeming too good to be true

FAKE ONLINE SHOPPING WARNING SIGNS

- Prices significantly lower than competitors
- Poor website design, broken English, and grammar errors
- No physical address or contact information for customer service
- Only accepts wire transfers, gift cards, or cryptocurrency
- No customer reviews or only fake-looking reviews
- Pressure to buy immediately with countdown timers

How to Protect Yourself

- Always check the URL carefully before entering sensitive information
- Look for HTTPS (the padlock icon) in your browser
- Never click links in suspicious emails
- Type website addresses directly into your browser

How to Protect Yourself

Use credit cards or PayPal for online purchases. These offer better fraud protection than debit cards, wire transfers, or gift cards. Check payment app policies before determining if they're a good fit.

> Congratulations User!
>
> We have specially selected you to receive rewards for your loyalty.
>
> This gift is exclusive to our users in California.
>
> Click OK to confirm.
>
> CLOSE

POP-UP SCAMS

Pop-up scams on cell phones and desktop computers are deceptive tactics used by cybercriminals to trick users into revealing personal information, installing malware, or paying for fake services. These scams often appear as alarming messages claiming your device is infected with a virus or has been hacked. They typically impersonate trusted brands like Apple, Microsoft, or antivirus providers, using official-looking logos and urgent language to create panic.

On iPhones, users might encounter fake "Apple Security Alerts" while browsing, warning that their device has been compromised. These pop-ups often prompt users to tap a link or call a support number. However, Apple does not send virus alerts via pop-ups—these are entirely fraudulent. Interacting with such messages can lead to phishing sites or malicious downloads.

Desktop users face similar threats, especially through fake tech support scams. These pop-ups claim to detect malware or system failures and urge users to call a support line. Once connected, scammers may request remote access to the computer or demand payment for unnecessary services. Some pop-ups even hijack the browser, making it difficult to close the warning without following the scam's instructions.

To protect yourself, avoid clicking on suspicious pop-ups, enable pop-up blockers, and keep your browser and security software updated. If you receive a warning, close the browser tab and clear your browsing data. Never call the number or download anything from these alerts. Awareness and caution are your best defenses against these increasingly sophisticated scams.

CAPTCHA SCAM

CAPTCHA* (Completely Automated Public Turing test to tell Computers and Humans Apart) is a security tool designed to distinguish between human users and automated bots. It's commonly used on websites to prevent spam, fraud, and unauthorized access by requiring users to complete simple tasks like identifying images or typing distorted text.

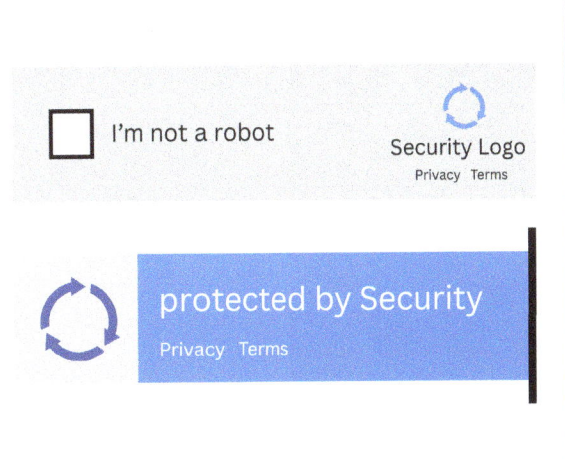

Similarly, reCAPTCHA™* is Google's security service to help websites distinguish between human users and automated bots. You can safely view a sample of a legitimate reCAPTCHA™ prompt here: *https://www.google.com/recaptcha/api2/demo*.

THE SCAM

CAPTCHA scams are deceptive traps where cybercriminals mimic legitimate CAPTCHA tests—those "I'm not a robot" challenges we sometimes see on websites we visit—to trick users into revealing personal information or downloading malware. These fake CAPTCHAs often appear on unfamiliar or suspicious websites and may redirect users to phishing pages or prompt unusual actions like downloading files or entering sensitive data.

RED FLAGS

Red flags include poor grammar, urgent language, unexpected pop-ups, or CAPTCHAs that ask for more than simple verification. To avoid falling victim, only interact with CAPTCHAs on trusted sites, keep your browser and security software updated, and never download anything from a CAPTCHA prompt.

WHAT TO DO IF YOU CLICK THE WRONG THING

If you suspect you've been duped, immediately close the page, run a malware scan using security software, change your passwords, and monitor your accounts for suspicious activity. Staying alert and skeptical is your best defense against these increasingly sophisticated scams.

Illustrative CAPTCHA- and reCAPTCHA-style images created by the author for educational use.

TRAVEL SCAMS & SAFETY

HOTEL DIGITAL KEYS

Accessing hotel rooms with digital keys is convenient but dangerous if your device isn't secure. Use of hotel wifi is unsecure. Hackers can sit at the bar or in the parking lot gaining access through unsecured wifi or by hacking through it or Bluetooth. Personal safety should be prioritized over free and convenient. If they hack your phone, they have your room key.

RENTAL CAR INFOTAINMENT SYSTEMS

Connecting cell phones to a rental car's infotainment system is convenient for calls, maps and music, but far too many return the car without deleting their device from the vehicle's system. Many cars store the contacts, call logs, text message history, GPS locations and home address even after you disconnect and return the car. When the company sells the vehicle, the new owner can extract data from the system. You must take the step to wipe your device from the vehicle to avoid the next renters from visibility to it.

PUBLIC CELL PHONE CHARGING

Scammers modify in-car infotainment systems and charging stations – like airport or public charging stations. Plugging in specifically via USB (vs. charging cord into outlet) can expose your phone to data extraction or malware installs while you think it's "just charging." It's safer to invest in an external charger to carry with you.

VIDEO GAME INTERNET CONNECTIVITY

Online video games offer thrilling adventures, social interaction, and endless entertainment—but when connected to the internet, they can also open the door to scams and serious risks. As gaming communities grow, so do the opportunities for cybercriminals to exploit unsuspecting players. One of the most common threats is **phishing**, where scammers send fake messages or emails that appear to be from game developers or platforms. These messages often urge players to "verify" their accounts or claim they've won rewards, tricking them into revealing login credentials.

Another danger lies in **in-game currency scams**. Players may encounter websites or users offering free or discounted virtual currency in exchange for personal information. These offers are almost always fraudulent and can lead to identity theft or financial loss. Additionally, downloading **unauthorized mods or cheat codes** can be risky. While they promise enhanced gameplay, many are laced with malware that can infect devices, steal data, or compromise security.

Young gamers are especially vulnerable, often unaware of the tactics scammers use to make contact while unsupervised. Fake sponsorships, rigged giveaways, and impersonation schemes are designed to exploit their excitement and trust. As online gaming continues to evolve, staying informed and cautious is essential. Players should use strong passwords, enable two-factor authentication, and avoid clicking suspicious links or downloading files from unverified sources. In the digital world of gaming, awareness is the best defense. Educating young gamers to these scams is a wise move.

INVESTMENT & CRYPTO SCAMS

WARNING SIGNS

- Guaranteed high returns with no risk
- Pressure to invest immediately
- Requests for upfront fees or personal information
- Unregistered investment opportunities
- Complex strategies that aren't clearly explained
- Testimonials from paid actors or celebrities (often fake)
- Requests to recruit friends, family, & new investors
- Difficulty withdrawing money
- Consistent returns regardless of market conditions

INVESTMENT SAFETY

Only invest through registered, regulated platforms. Research any investment thoroughly and never invest money you can't afford to lose. If it sounds too good to be true, it probably is.

Over $1b is lost annually to crypto scams.

CRYPTO SCAM TYPES

- Fake cryptocurrency exchanges
- Pump and dump schemes
- Fake celebrity crypto giveaways
- Romance scams involving crypto
- Fake crypto investment sites/platforms
- Monitor for new & evolving schemes

INVESTMENT SCAMS	CRYPTO SCAMS	PONZI SCHEMES
Investment scams promise high returns with little risk. They often use social media, fake celebrity endorsements, and pressure tactics.	Crypto schemes are particularly dangerous because transactions are irreversible and largely unregulated. Various schemes involving fake cryptocurrency exchanges, pump-and-dump schemes, or promises of guaranteed returns on crypto investments.	Investment scams that pay existing investors with money from new investors, creating the illusion of legitimate returns. They eventually collapse when new investors can't be found.

Romance scams target people looking for love, usually online. Scammers create fake profiles and build emotional relationships before asking for money for travel, emergencies, gifts, or other fabricated needs.

WARNING SIGNS

- Moves too fast – professes love very quickly
- Avoids phone calls or video chats
- Claims to be traveling, working overseas, or military deployed
- Has emergencies requiring immediate financial help
- Asks for money, gifts, or personal information
- Photos look too professional or model-like

VERIFICATION TIPS

Use reverse image search on profile photos. Be suspicious if someone can't video chat or meet in person. Never send money to someone you've only met online.

ROMANCE SCAMS

HOUSE & LAND THEFT

REAL ESTATE FRAUD

Real estate fraud involves deceptive practices like fake property listings, wire transfer scams, and forged ownership documents, often targeting buyers during high-stress moments, like closing. In 2022 alone, the FBI received over 11,000 real estate fraud complaints, totaling nearly $400 million in reported losses.

Theft of homes and land is on the rise to a point where many counties are implementing notification systems for residents to alert them to newly-recorded documents of sale, refinance or transfer attributed to their property – if the residents opt in.

While a positive step, by the time the resident learns of the issue, the scam is already in progress. Find out if there is a notification system available in your jurisdiction.

WHO'S MOST VULNERABLE

- Land owners who don't occupy the property full time to witness showings
- Property owners with paid-off mortgages – lenders and their army of attorneys are no longer engaged
- Seniors (60+) accounted for nearly half the losses in 2023

DOES TITLE INSURANCE PROTECT ME?

It depends on the policy. Most homeowners pay for a title policy at closing – but it was a *lender's* title insurance policy and not an *owner's* policy; the lender's policy ends when the mortgage is paid off. If you have an owner's policy for yourself, it likely covers forged deeds, past fraud, and legal defense. It can't stop fraud, may not cover new scams, and won't cover you if you are tricked into signing transaction documents.

It may be worth inquiring about an owner's title insurance policy. It is usually a one-time fee calculated as a percentage of the property's value – generally 0.5% to 1% – and has optional endorsements available. Rates are regulated by most states, so costs can vary depending on where you live. For best advice in your state, consult an attorney.

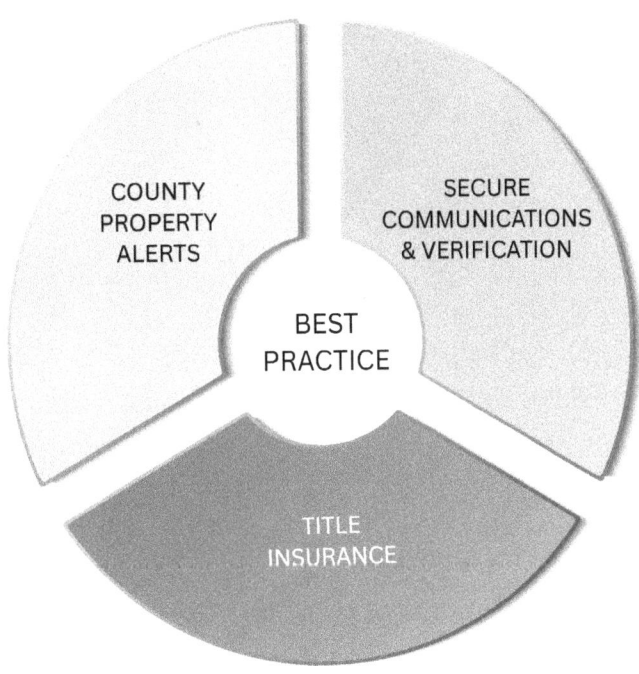

COUNTY PROPERTY ALERTS

SECURE COMMUNICATIONS & VERIFICATION

BEST PRACTICE

TITLE INSURANCE

COMMON SCAMS

NIGERIAN PRINCE SCAM

This is a classic advance-fee fraud begun in the 1990s where someone claims to be royalty or a wealthy individual who needs help transferring money, promising a large reward for your assistance.

Modern Variations Include:

- Lottery winnings you never entered
- Inheritance from unknown relatives
- Business partnership opportunities
- Charity scams after disasters

BANK SCAM

Emails that appear to be from your bank, claiming there's a problem with your account and asking you to click a link to verify your information. Emails may claim to be from a bank employee or fraud department.

How to Verify:

- Check the sender's email address carefully
- Look for spelling and grammar errors
- Don't click links - go directly to your bank's website
- Call your bank using the number on your card

DELIVERY SCAM

Fake emails claiming to be from shipping companies like FedEx, UPS, or Amazon saying there's a problem with a delivery and asking you to click a link or download an attachment to provide better address information or to reschedule a delivery.

Safety Tips:

- Assess if you're actually expecting a package
- Don't download attachments from unknown senders
- Use official tracking numbers on company websites
- Be wary of urgent language and threats

BRUSHING SCAM

This scam also includes a delivery of an unexpected package in the mail. The parcel may be in envelope or package form and may claim to be from familiar retailers. Inside is a QR code for you to scan. Like other scams, it may claim to be a "reward" or way for you to "thank the sender" for their thoughtful gift. Scanning this code immediately directs your device to a scam website set up to steal personal or financial information. Some QR codes install malware onto devices.

Safety Tips:
- Mail and parcels with this appearance should be discarded.
- If you didn't order something from the shipping retailer, treat it as suspicious.
- If you have an online account with the shipping retailer, check your account for unauthorized purchases.
- If you did scan the code and entered personal information, change account passwords, review account activity for fraud, and run virus software on your devices.

REFUND APPROVAL SCAM

Fake texts or emails claiming to be a local, county, state or federal jurisdiction advising you of a refund due. The sender may claim to be from a department of taxation or any official corporate or government entity urging you to click the accompanying link. The link may include "gov" but isn't from a ".gov" address. This is another attempt to engage and should be met with deletion. Red Flags include fake links and senders using vague entity names. Customers and taxpayers can verify through legitimate means if they are owed a refund

ONLINE REAL ESTATE LISTING SCAM

Fake apartment or housing listings and ads which look legitimate and appealing, often with photos and videos. They are posted by scammers impersonating licensed real estate agents and usually include imagery of actual listings advertised with below-market rates. The intent is to lure interested parties to submit an application with personal information along with a steep application fee.

Safety Tips:
- Watch for common red flags including rates too good to be true and urgency to not miss a limited opportunity.
- Research market rates and standard application fees so you're armed with the ability to question costs.
- Avoid paying any fee for a property unseen.
- Contact the realtor using information you've looked up independently (not from the listing or from a search engine search result).

TRUST
but
VERIFY

CHAPTER

07

FAMILY
SAFETY
TACTICS

The best way to stay secure and keep those in our world safe is to share... Scam attempts, defense tactics, and new ideas to stay one step ahead of fraud.

FRAUD SAFE FAMILY AWARENESS GAMES & ACTIVITIES

In the spirit of practicing what we preach – as schools conduct drills and businesses test employees with fake emails – consider that open discussion is often the best way to learn and share experiences.

It would be easy and fun – and different – to incorporate some fraud awareness activities into your next pizza or game night. Certainly, family members of all ages would walk away more confident and capable.

SCAM BINGO

Create bingo cards with common scam red flags (e.g., "Too good to be true," "Urgent request," "Unknown number," "Pay in gift cards"). As you talk through real examples, family members mark their squares. First to yell "Fraud Wise!" wins.

INTERGENERATIONAL "WHAT WOULD YOU DO?" DISCUSSION

Each generation brings a story: For kids, maybe an online gaming "friend" asking for something. For parents, email, text or scam attempts you recognized; and for grandparents, phone or mail scams. Compare how each person would respond, then agree on a "family fraud rule."

"REAL OR FAKE?" CHALLENGE

Print or project screenshots of sample texts, emails, or social media posts (mix in both real promotions and scam messages). Each family member votes "real" or "fake." Discuss why they made that choice—helps sharpen critical thinking.

SPOT THE SCAM RELAY

Split into teams. Each round, a short scenario is read aloud (like a phone call from "the IRS" or a Facebook friend asking for money). Teams race to buzz in with the scam clue (e.g., "Government doesn't call!"). Quick, high-energy, great for all ages.

PASSWORD STRENGTH CONTEST

Everyone writes down a password they might use. Use a free online password strength checker (or a chart of what makes a password strong). Kids love trying to "outsmart" the adults with the strongest one.

FRAUD SAFE TRIVIA

Split into teams. Each round, a short scenario is read aloud (like a phone call from "the IRS" or a Facebook friend asking for money). Teams race to buzz in with the scam clue (e.g., "Government doesn't call!"). Quick, high-energy, great for all ages.

ROLE-PLAY SCENARIOS

Kids pretend to be scammers using silly voices ("You've won a free giraffe!"). Parents or grandparents practice spotting the trick and responding.Great way to teach kids how scams *sound* and how to say "No thanks".

Family
BRAINSTORM

Families should regularly come together to assess digital security because open conversations help everyone understand the risks and stay informed about evolving threats. Every generation in the family can share experiences—like spotting phishing emails or setting up strong passwords—empowers each member to protect themselves and others. When digital safety becomes a shared responsibility, it builds trust and creates a stronger, smarter household defense.

If your cell phone became lost or stolen would you know what to do? Discuss the steps you'd take and rehearse them!

Research yourself. Search to find open-source on each other to understand how scammers could have that info.

Compare and discuss phone apps. Understand if each has access to your location, camera, photos & microphone, then discuss the pros and cons.

Discuss all home connected devices including smart TVs, thermostats, doorbells, Echo Dot and Google cloud assistants, & health wearables to assess privacy and understand vulnerabilities.

THINK LIKE AN INVESTIGATOR

BE YOUR OWN CONSUMER ADVOCATE

Prepare for Scammer Contact. You don't need a gold badge to have and use your analytical skills.

It's not a matter of if, but when, the next scam will come. Think ahead, and pause to consider:

- Who
- What
- When
- Why
- How
- Where

REHEARSE	MAKE TIME	SUMMON COURAGE
what your responses may be – including not answering or hanging up!	and maintain composure during calls and text & email reviews. The moment is yours; make decisions at your own pace. Stay calm, actively listen, pause & reflect; avoid pressure to be rushed.	Remember you are the important half of the conversation; you're the one who's actually in control.

Trust your instincts. If something feels wrong or too good to be true, take time to research and verify. Scammers rely on pressure, emotion & urgency - **slow down and think critically** before taking any action involving money or personal information. Ensure you have time to make informed, reasonable decisions.

- Use strong, unique passwords – passphrases are better – for all accounts
- Enable two-factor authentication when available
- Keep software and antivirus programs updated
- Regularly monitor your financial statements
- Review your credit report annually or if a problem is suspected
- Consider freezing your credit with all credit reporting agencies
- Federal employees: place a lock on your TSP account
- Be cautious about sharing personal information – come from a place of no!

FAMILY PLEDGES
&
FAMILY PASSWORDS

Step 1: Everyone agrees on a family password.
Step 2: Everyone writes one personal fraud-wise rule on a family page, or everyone writes their own page of "Fraud Safe" pledges that are updated annually. Hang them on the fridge or inside cabinet doors for visibility and reminder.

These activities balance fun with practicality and ensure that kids, parents, and grandparents all *leave game night wiser*. Beyond the topic of fraud, nights like these turn into great bonding experiences and memories.

*it takes
a village,
ask
someone
trusted*

SMART DEVICE CORE FEATURES

"Smart" in the context of devices doesn't just mean clever or trendy. It refers to a set of technical capabilities that make a device more interactive, autonomous, and connected than traditional electronics.

WHAT MAKES THEM SMART

Connectivity: They connect to other devices or networks via Wi-Fi, Bluetooth, 5G, or other protocols.

Sensors: They gather data from the environment—like motion, temperature, location, or biometrics.

Processing Power: They have built-in computing ability to analyze data and make decisions.

Autonomy: They can perform tasks automatically or respond to user behavior without constant input.

Interactivity: They respond to voice, touch, or other inputs and often personalize their behavior.

Integration: They sync with apps, cloud platforms, or other smart systems for seamless control.

In short, "smart" means the device is part of the Internet of Things (IoT)—a network of connected gadgets that can communicate, learn, and act on their own. But with all that intelligence comes risk: more data, more connections, and more opportunities for scams or breaches. For these reasons, it's important to keep **device software and firmware routinely updated**, **avoid third-party apps** unless verified, and regularly **review privacy settings and data-sharing permissions**. Convenience comes with responsibility.

PASSKEYS & BANKING SECURITY

Passkeys are emerging as a powerful alternative to traditional passwords, offering a secure, phishing-resistant way to access online accounts. A digital credential, passkeys use device-based credentials—like biometrics or PINs—without transmitting secrets over the internet. Banks are beginning to adopt passkeys to reduce fraud and streamline logins. Because passkeys are stored securely on users' devices and synced across platforms like iCloud Keychain or Google Password Manager, they offer both enhanced protection and a smoother user experience.

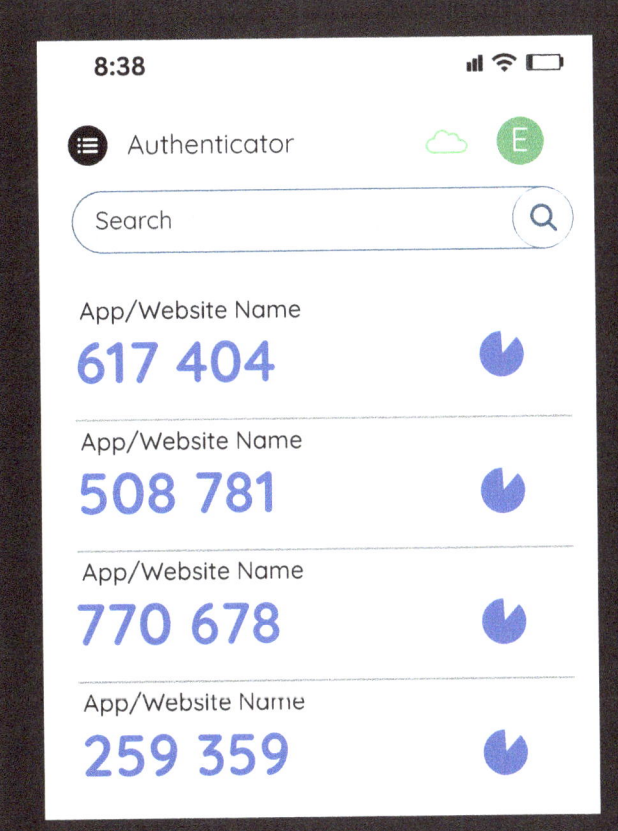

2FA AUTHENTICATOR APPS

These add a critical layer of security through multi-factor authentication (MFA), generating time-based one-time passcodes (OTP) that refresh every 30 seconds. Apps like Microsoft Authenticator, Google Authenticator, and 2FA ensure that even if a password is compromised, unauthorized access is blocked without the second factor. These apps store secret keys locally and use encryption, making them resistant to phishing and SIM-swapping attacks. Lightweight, easy to use, and often free, authenticator apps are a smart upgrade for anyone serious about protecting their digital identity.

smart devices

PERSONAL ELECTRONICS & DEVICES

Smartphones & Tablets – Most common targets for phishing, malware, and fake apps.

Laptops & Desktops – Vulnerable to ransomware, spyware, and malicious downloads.

Smart Watches & Fitness Trackers – Can leak health data or location if not secured.

Wireless Headphones & Earbuds – Some models have voice assistants or location tracking.

E-Readers & Smart Pens – Often overlooked but may store personal data or connect to cloud services.

Smart Glasses & Lenses

HOME & APPLIANCES

Smart TVs – Can be used to track viewing habits or serve malicious ads.

Smart Speakers (e.g., Alexa, Google Home) – Always listening; vulnerable to voice spoofing.

Smart Thermostats & Lights – Can be hacked to track your presence or routines.

Smart Door Locks & Security Systems – Critical to secure; a breach could mean physical access.

Smart Smoke/CO Detectors – May fail to alert if software is outdated or tampered with.

Smart Plugs & Outlets – Can be used to manipulate devices remotely.

Baby Monitors & Child Trackers – Often targeted for surveillance or data theft.

VEHICLES

Connected Cars – GPS, infotainment systems, and remote start features can be hacked.

Bluetooth & Wi-Fi in Vehicles – Entry points for attackers if not properly secured.

Dash Cams & Vehicle Cameras – May store footage in the cloud or transmit data externally.

WEARABLES & HEALTH TECH

Smart Glasses & AR/VR Headsets – Can record surroundings or transmit sensitive data.

Medical Wearables (e.g., glucose monitors, heart rate sensors) – Often connected to apps or cloud services.

Smart PPE (Personal Protective Equipment) – Used in workplaces; may transmit biometric or environmental data.

TOYS & ENTERTAINMENT

Connected Toys & Dolls – Some have microphones, cameras, or GPS.

Gaming Consoles & Online Games – Can be used for scams, phishing, or social engineering.

TRAVEL & LIFESTYLE TECH

Smart Luggage – GPS tracking and app control can be exploited.

Smart Water Bottles, Mirrors, or Scales – Often sync with apps and collect personal data.

GENERAL SETTINGS

- Set a strong lock screen (PIN, password, fingerprint, or face ID). Avoid easy codes like 1234 or birthdays.
- Enable Auto-Lock (30 sec–1 min).
- Turn on 'Find My Device' (Apple: Find My iPhone / Android: Find My Device); know login info in case your device is ever stolen for immediate tracking or remote default reset.
- Install software updates promptly to patch security flaws.

WIRELESS CONNECTIONS

- Bluetooth: Turn off when not in use. Set to 'Non-discoverable' or 'Contacts Only'.
- Wi-Fi: Disable 'Auto-Join Public Networks'. Use trusted, password-protected Wi-Fi. Consider a VPN on public hotspots.
- AirDrop (Apple): Set to 'Contacts Only' or 'Off' (never 'Everyone').
- Hotspot/Tethering: Use a strong password. Turn off when not in use.

PRIVACY & PERMISSIONS

- Review app permissions (location, microphone, camera, contacts). Deny unnecessary access.
- Location Services: Set to 'While Using App' instead of 'Always'.
- Turn off location sharing when not needed.
- Limit Ad Tracking (Apple) / Opt Out of Ads Personalization (Android).

SHARING & BACKUPS

- Enable automatic backups (iCloud, Google Drive).
- Turn on Two-Factor Authentication (2FA) for email, banking, shopping apps.
- Enable alerts for new logins to accounts.

FRAUD-SAFE COLLECTIVE FAMILY TIPS

- Never share login info
- Never accept random Bluetooth or AirDrop requests.
- Be careful where you plug your device in to charge; use electrical outlet instead of USB into an public or unverified charging station.
- Keep 2FA enabled for banking/shopping accounts.
- Review permissions and turn off Wi-Fi/Bluetooth when not in use.
- Review other phone settings that may add protection.

BE CAUTIONS WITH CALLS, EMAIL & TEXTS

Don't be pressured & don't click links or attachments unless you've assessed they're safe. Look at sender (do you do business with them?) & sender email (does it look legitimate?) If it's legitimate, you can contact the source directly, get the sale, or accomplish the goal an alternate way.

AVOID PUBLIC WIFI & UNSECURED NETWORKS

Anything you access on an unsecured network is open to theft. Bring or pay for encrypted wifi & avoid the convenience of "free" at hotels, coffee shops, etc. It's not free if you're hacked.

USE STRONG & UNIQUE PASSWORDS/PHRASES

Instead of a word, number and other character, use a phrase. Example: "IlovedmyvacationtoOrlandoin#2019". Studies show scammers' password-hacking software doesn't do as well with phrases. Consider a phrase using the first letter in a string of words; like above: "ILMVTO#2019." Or allow an authenticator app to generate a passcode.
Agree on a family-only password

MONITOR BANK & CREDIT ACCOUNTS

Regularly & immediately question or report any amount you can't verify as yours. Your bank/credit terms of service limit the window of time in which you can report fraud and receive restitution. You get a free credit report annually – take advantage of that!

ENGAGE MULTI-FACTOR AUTHENTICATION

On all accounts – it may insert a delay of a few seconds but is like an insurance policy of sorts & worth it.

SHRED SENSITIVE DOCUMENTS

Shred before discarding (financial, medical, tax, Social Security, pharmacy, etc.).

PRACTICAL RESOURCES

Refers to the act of gaining unauthorized access to or control over a digital device – like a smartphone, computer, tablet, or even smart TVs, security cameras, video gaming systems, thermostats, and appliances – for:

- Data theft of personal, financial or work information
- Surveillance to monitor your activity or location
- Sabotage to disable or corrupt systems
- Monetary gain through ransomware, fraud, or selling stolen data

HOW IT HAPPENS

- Rooting/jailbraking to modify the device operating system to bypass manufacturer restrictions
- Remote Access Trojans (RATs) is malware allowing a hacker to control a device remotely
- Network-based attacks exploit vulnerable wifi & Bluetooth
- Physical Access Hacking is plugging into other devices (or hacked charging stations) to bypass passwords
- Firmware exploits target the low-level software controlling hardware & can permanently compromise it
- Mobile service provider account hack (account & phone number takeover)
- Hack via Bluetooth, unsecured public network or fake business wifi that looks real

WARNING SIGNS

Hacked devices often show subtle or obvious signs of a potential problem, including:

Smart Phones & Tablets

- Rapidly draining battery
- Overheating
- Unfamiliar apps and/or settings
- Pop-ups & ads
- Data usage spikes
- Messages sent without your knowledge

Computers & Laptops

- Slow performance – lagging/freezing
- Unusual network activity & crashing
- Disabled antivirus software or firewall
- Strange files or programs
- Mouse/cursor moves on its own
- Browser redirects

Other Smart Devices

- Lights, sounds or cameras trigger unexpectedly
- Unauthorized access logs
- Firmware updates you didn't initiate
- Video gaming system contact

IDENTITY THEFT

This is when scammers have enough data to take over any type of email, social media or financial account without our permission; they do it with data stolen or illicitly solicited from us as part of a scheme. It can include:

- Takeover of existing financial or social media accounts
- Opening new accounts (credit cards, loans)
- Accessing your bank and/or email accounts
- Filing false tax returns to obtain refund
- Receiving medical services under your name

HOW IT HAPPENS

Scammers cast a wide net by using computers, programs & teams to work quickly by sending:

- Phishing emails or fake websites & links that trick us into giving up important data
- Skimming devices hidden in plain site on ATMs, gas pumps, & retailer pay kiosks
- Oversharing on social media
- Using public wifi to connect your devices
- Dumpster diving for discarded documents & statements

⚑ WARNING SIGNS

Scammers cast a wide net by using computers & teams to work quickly by sending:

- Bills for things you didn't buy
- Debt collection calls for unknown accounts
- Denied credit applications
- Missing mail or unexpected address changes
- Sudden inundation with emails (email bomb)

KNOWLEDGE

is

POWER

WHERE TO FIND HELP

Immediate Goals:

If you find you've been scammed, don't panic – you're in good company. Your priorities now are **stopping the hack**, **reporting**, **documentation**, and **to be made whole financially.**

1

1. **Stop all communication with the scammer(s).**
2. **Assess the Big Picture** – Assess if your incident exposed anyone else and immediately warn them.
3. Secure any accounts you know were affected, then move to secure other accounts which could still be impacted.
4. Start from the affected account then assess each account in order of account importance.
5. Contact financial institutions and pause or freeze credit cards if impacted.
6. Create/access credit reporting bureau accounts to place a fraud alert (Equifax, Experian & TransUnion).

2

Local Police Report – Report the incident to your local police department and obtain a copy of the report.
- Provide information on your steps following the incident – documentation of this could be important later.
- The level of assistance they can provide depends on the scam type; ask for their advice and for available resources.

3

Insurance Coverage – Check your coverages and make a report to all providers – submit a copy of your police report.
- Consider all coverages before filing a claim – determine which best fits the incident. Many policies have specific endorsements and exclusions for "digital assets" (like cryptocurrency) and "electronic vandalism."
- Think ID theft protection insurance, coverage through work or retail breaches, and many homeowners' insurance policies have standard coverage.

WHERE TO FIND HELP

Once you've taken the preceding initial steps, consider this comprehensive list* of places (in order of priority contact) you can report scams in the U.S., including national agencies, specialized services, and key helplines:

Federal & National Reporting Resources

Federal Trade Commission (FTC)
Online: Report any scam, fraud, or bad business practice at ReportFraud.ftc.gov
Phone: 1-877-382-4357 (FTC-HELP)

Internet Crime Complaint Center (IC3)
Online: IC3.gov (part of the FBI) to report internet- and cyber-related scams, including phishing, romance scams, business email compromise, and cryptocurrency fraud

Federal Bureau of Investigation (FBI)
Online: Submit tips or complaint via fbi.gov/tips, or contact your local FBI field office

U.S. Postal Inspection Service
Online: Report mail-based scams like fake checks, sweepstakes, reshipping schemes, or mail fraud

Consumer Financial Protection Bureau (CFPB)
Phone: Report financial, credit, or loan-related scams at 855-411-2372

Treasury Inspector General for Tax Administration (TIGTA)
Phone: Report IRS-related phishing or tax scams; the same 800-366-4484 number is used for USPS scams

U.S. Department of Health & Human Services (HHS) — Office of Inspector General (OIG)
Phone: Report Medicare or Medicaid fraud to the OIG at at 800-HHS-TIPS / 800-447-8477

Securities and Exchange Commission (SEC)
Online: Report investment or securities fraud via SEC's online reporting tools at SEC.gov

State Attorney General / State Consumer Protection Office
Report scams—especially local or business-related—to your state Attorney General's office; most have hotlines or complaint forms

USA.gov
Use the site to find the best place to report based on your specific situation

WHERE TO FIND HELP

Specialized Helplines & Support

Identity Theft Resource Center (ITRC)
Phone: 1-888-400-5530 — Free support for identity theft victims

AARP Fraud Watch Network Helpline
Phone: 1-877-908-3360 — Support and referrals for elders and families
Also offers education, scam alerts, and emotional support groups

National Elder Fraud Hotline
Phone: 1-833-372-8311 — Dedicated to seniors and elder financial fraud victims

Victim Connect Resource Center
Phone: 1-855-484-2846 — Connects victims to local counseling and resources

Communications-Specific Reporting

Phone Scams & Robocalls
FTC Phone: 1-877-382-4357
FCC: Report at 1-888-225-5322 or file a complaint online

Text (SMS) Scams
Forward spam texts to: 7726 ("SPAM") where carriers may block the sender

Email / Phishing
Forward to APWG: reportphishing@apwg.org
Bank phishing: Also forward to spam@uce.gov and notify the real company being impersonated
IRS phishing: Report to phishing@irs.gov

WHERE TO FIND HELP

Real Estate Fraud & Title Theft

1. **Go to the County Registry of Deeds** – immediately obtain a copy of the fraudulent documents and advise the clerk's office of the fraud.
2. **File a Police Report** – report the fraud to police and provide a copy of the fraudulent ownership documents you received from the county.
3. **Call the District Attorney or State Attorney General** – report to any real estate fraud unit and provide a copies of the police report and fraudulent documents.
4. **Seek Legal Counsel** – immediately speak to a real estate attorney for assistance with next steps.
5. **File with the FBI-IC3** – file a complaint if it's determined wire fraud, phishing, or online impersonation is involved.
6. **Contact the FTC** – file a complaint of identity theft or impersonation.

Missing or Stolen Device Emergency Checklist

Follow these steps immediately if your device is lost or stolen.
Steps are ordered from simplest actions to worst-case scenario.

- Stay calm and assess if the phone is lost or stolen or simply misplaced.
- Try calling or messaging your phone.
- Lock your device remotely (iPhone: Find My iPhone, Android: Find My Device).
- Track the phone's location if safe; share with police if help is needed.
- Change important passwords (email, banking, Apple ID/Google account, social media).
- Remove payment options (Apple Pay, Google Wallet, credit/debit cards).
- Notify your mobile carrier to suspend service; provide IMEI/serial number.
- File a police report with device details.
- Wipe the device remotely if recovery is unlikely.
- Monitor accounts for suspicious activity.
- Replace your phone and restore from backup if necessary.

Extra Tips:
- Enable two-factor authentication on all accounts.
- Regularly back up your phone.
- Keep your device passcode-protected.
- Use tracking apps and remote-wipe features proactively.

ADVANCE FEE SCAM

Scammers promise money, prizes, or jobs but demand an upfront payment (e.g., lottery scams, inheritance scams).

BLUEJACKING

A Bluetooth based attack where a message is sent to you by an unknown sender using Bluetooth.

BLUESNARFING

A Bluetooth based attack where a hacker connects to your device via Bluetooth.

COMPUTER HARDWARE

The physical components of a computer system that you can see and touch.

COMPUTER SOFTWARE

The programs and apps that tell a computer, phone, or tablet what to do.

DATA BREACH

When hackers steal personal or financial information from a company's database.

DEEPFAKE

A fake video, image, or audio created using artificial intelligence that looks or sounds real (to impersonate someone).

E-MAIL BLAST/BOMB/FLOOD

When scammers inundate your email with spam as a hacked 2FA or MFA code is expected, so as to distract you from the hack. Also known as an Email Flood.

IDENTITY THEFT

When someone uses your personal details (like Social Security number or credit card) to steal money or open accounts.

INTERNET OF THINGS (IOT)

Refers to the growing network of physical devices that are connected to the internet, collecting and exchanging data automatically.

INVESTMENT SCAM

Fake opportunities (crypto, stocks, gold, etc.) promising big returns with little risk.

ISP

Internet Service Provider (like Comcast, AT&T)

JUICE JACKING

A cyberattack of a public charging station a modified USB cable/port to steal data or install malware.

MALVERTISING

An attempt to get a user to click on an ad without thinking; the ad looks real but is malicious.

MALWARE

Harmful software installed on your device to steal data or spy on you.

MULTI-FACTOR AUTHENTICATION (MFA)

A security method that requires two or more proofs of identity before letting you log in (password + code)

PASSWORD MANAGER

A tool that creates and stores strong, unique passwords so you don't have to remember them all.

PHISHING

Fake emails, texts, or messages that trick you into clicking a link or giving personal information.

PIG BUTCHERING SCAM

A newer online scam where fraudsters gain trust over time, then trick people into fake investments (often crypto).

PRETEXTING OR SIM SWAPPING

Impersonation of a user with the phone company.

RANSOMWARE

Malicious software that locks your files and demands payment to unlock them.

RED FLAG

A warning sign something might be a scam (e.g., urgency, secrecy, asking for gift cards).

ROMANCE SCAM

Fraudsters pretend to build a relationship online or by phone, then ask for money or favors.

SKIMMING

A device attached to ATMs, gas pumps or card readers that steals your credit/debit card information.

SMISHING

A scam sent by text message (SMS), often pretending to be from a bank, delivery service, or government agency.

SOCIAL ENGINEERING

Tricks that use human emotions — like fear, urgency, or greed — to manipulate people into giving away information.

SPOOFING

When scammers disguise their phone number or email address to make it look like it's coming from someone you trust.

TECH SUPPORT SCAM

A fraud where scammers pretend to be computer/software support (often claiming to be from Microsoft, Apple, or your ISP).

TWO-FACTOR AUTHENTICATION (2FA)

"2FA" is an extra security step requiring a code (sent to your phone or app) along with your password.

VISHING

Fraudulent phone calls ("voice phishing") where scammers impersonate officials, banks, or tech support.

WIFI ENTRY

A successful hack of a device through unsecured or public wifi.

GLOSSARY

CHANCE FAVORS THE PREPARED MIND

THANK you

Acknowledgements

i am deeply grateful to my extraordinary parents — Always my true North. My mother, who instilled in me a deep appreciation for language, grammar, and the elegance of thoughtfulness, expression and etiquette. And my father, who cultivated and sharpened my analytical mind, teaching me to evaluate, think critically, and solve creatively. Your unwavering encouragement, steadfast support, and invaluable lessons shaped not only the person I am today but also the foundation of a fulfilling career in public service — which has, in turn, allowed me to positively impact the lives of others. This stands as a testament to the love, faith, knowledge and inspiration you have always generously given — gifts that guide my every step.

My heartfelt thanks to my amazing sister Barbara — A brilliant mind, a boundless talent, and a sense of humor that brings bright light. Your dogged support, laughter, and kindness have shaped my life in countless ways. This is a tribute to your creativity, your wisdom, and the joy you bring. You are the consummate designer and font whisperer whose perfect Boston accent makes everything sound smahtah. Heah we ahh!

In loving memory — of my amazing grandparents, who were so generous with their love, support, encouragement, and interest in everything I did. And of Randy, and MBD. Your spirit I carry with me. And of the generations before them I've come to know and admire through genealogy.

With love and appreciation to my best friends through the years — sincerest thanks to Jennifer, Lorna, Cheryl, Brenda, Lorraine, Jody, Wendy, Arlene, and Pam.

I wish to extend my sincerest appreciation to all the people who helped me along my path in public service — The mentors who guided me, the colleagues who inspired me, the friends who encouraged me, and those who allowed me opportunities to swerve out of my lane to learn more and do more. Your support, wisdom, investment and integrity shaped my journey and steered my course. Special thanks to Joe, Kevin, Billy, Jeremy, Sean, Randy, Keith, Dave, Shirley, Ron, Terry, Katie, Mike, Doug, Andy, Rich, and Kathy.

I'm profoundly grateful to federal ethics expert and former Inspector General Mark Greenblatt for lending your voice to this project; your generous testimonial and kind words added weight and warmth to the message I hoped to share. Among the outstanding IGs I've worked for, your leadership style left a lasting impression as being uniquely effective in inspiring those around you to rise to their highest potential. Indeed, our trajectory was (and is) straight up.

To all those who have worked or are working in public safety — thank you for your service. At every level, you are the front lines in the US. Thank you for working midnights, doubles and holidays. For walking – running – toward the danger, the flames, the darkness, the BS, and the unknown. Thank you for doing what can feel like a thankless job – may the "calling" and the personal reward it brings make up for the rest.

I'm forever grateful, and "Always giving thanks to God the Father for everything." –Ephesians 5:20

PREVENT. DETECT. PROTECT.